WOMEN

MAXIM'S UNAUTHORIZED GUIDE

WOMEN

MAXIM'S UNAUTHORIZED GUIDE

CATCH HER EYE SCORE THAT FIRST DATE SEDUCE HER GET HER NAKED

ROMANCE HER FIGURE HER OUT WIN HER OVER DRIVE HER WILD

BY THE EDITORS OF MAXIM

MAXIM
BOOKS

DDM Press

DDM PRESS 1040 Avenue of the Americas New York, NY 10018

212.302.2626 http://www.maximmag.com

ISBN 0-9675723-3-9 (hardcover)
ISBN 0-9675723-0-4 (softcover)
Printed in the United States of America

WOMEN: **MAXIM'S UNAUTHORIZED GUIDE**

SENIOR EDITOR LESLIE YAZEL
DESIGN DIRECTOR KAREN J
PHOTOGRAPHER PHILLIP WONG
PHOTO EDITOR LORETTA BLACK
DESIGN ASSISTANT CAROL ANN BURTON
PRODUCTION/RETOUCHING MICHELLE CIULLA, OMAR RAWLISON
CHAPTER EDITORS CARMEN ARMILLAS, DAWN YANEK
WRITERS EILEEN WILDE, KIMBERLY FLYNN
COPY EDITOR TOM BROWN
RESEARCHER CAROLINE BOLLINGER
DIGITAL ENHANCEMENT GENE BRESLER
STYLIST EVAN ROSS
PRODUCTION ASSISTANT JEREMY RIZZI
HAIR AND MAKEUP SCOTT SUMMERS
THANKS TO BAR LOCATION ANTARCTICA BAR, NYC

DDM Press

CHAIRMAN FELIX DENNIS
PRESIDENT STEPHEN COLVIN
CHIEF FINANCIAL OFFICER PAUL FISH
PUBLISHER STEVEN KOTOK
GROUP CREATIVE DIRECTOR KEITH BLANCHARD
PRODUCTION MANAGER LOU TERRACCIANO
DIRECT MARKETING MANAGER JOANNA MOLFETTA
DIRECTORS ROBERT G. BARTNER,
PETER GODFREY

ACKNOWLEDGEMENT & THANKS
SPECIAL THANKS TO EVERYONE AT DENNIS PUBLISHING WHO CONSULTED,
ADVISED, CONTRIBUTED, SUPPORTED, AND TOLERATED
THE MANY ACTIVITIES SURROUNDING THE CREATION OF THIS BOOK.

CONTENTS

INTRO

You're probably not a rookie when it comes to the world of women. In fact, for all we know, you could be thriving on a steady diet of Victoria's Secret vixens, bisexual beauties, and gullible college coeds who say, "OK, fun!" when you ask them to put on their waitress uniforms and take your very special order. But in a world in which you're not dreaming, a little guidance can go a long way toward making the gentler gender less of a mind bender.

I think I speak for all women when I say that meeting, seducing, bedding, and (when you finally come around) wedding us can be surprisingly simple. We love sex just as much as you do, so it pains us to watch you fuck up easy opportunities to get us into bed. When a nice guy like you blows it, we sigh and say to each other over our frozen drinks, "Why is he making it all so hard? If only he had done such and such, we'd be bouncing around in his bed right now!"

That's why the editors of Maxim, *along with a team of experts, sexperts, and dozens of real women, have designed this book to supply you with everything you need to know about women: how to pick 'em up, how to wine and dine 'em, how to win fights with 'em, how to push their lust buttons. Let the girls and me show you how to attract women from 60 paces and how to transform your pad into a chick-friendly den of sin in 15 minutes. How to buy her the ultimate gift in the space of a commercial break. How to push her buttons so perfectly that deep-space satellites will register her screaming your name.*

Want more? We'll show you how to get forgiven for cheating, how to last longer in bed, and how to effortlessly persuade your gal to act out your most bizarre sexual fantasies right here, right now, oh yeah, baby. But hey, if all of the above is old hat to you, then by all means, go back to licorice-whipping your harem of supermodels while your wife cooks a steak dinner for you and your poker buddies. Everyone else, read on. Then come and get us, boys!

—**Leslie Yazel,** who incidentally has an unlisted phone number, was an editor at *Maxim* until she found a job for which she wasn't required to wear a French maid's uniform and bend over to pick up pencils off the floor.

chapter one

Catch Her Eye

A girl glances at you, then looks away and doesn't notice you for the rest of the night. What'd you do wrong? The girls and I are about to tell you...and we'll fix it so it doesn't happen again.

She could be a brilliant neurosurgeon, an accomplished jazz musician, a compassionate listener. But when you first lay eyes on her sitting at the next table, your first impression is likely to be more along the lines of "Whoa— nice rack!" Men's initial reactions are primal, simple, and to the point. We girls are cool with that; that's why that neurosurgeon gal's wearing the tube top.

But you need to understand that women's first impressions are anything but simple—there are no "dick girls" or "ass girls." She may look like she's casually glancing your way, but in reality her eyes are roving all over you like one of those Bond-film mini-spy-cams, and her brain's whirring like a high-speed supercomputer, taking a complex head-to-toe inventory involving megabytes of clear and specific information you had no idea you were revealing. No matter what the ads say, there simply isn't one perfect shirt or pick-up line or haircut or cologne that'll reel women in. Rather, it's the complicated interplay of all these things, plus a few intangibles we've actually managed to quantify in this chapter using state-of-the-art NASA technology, that makes her want you to come hither, baby.

As you'll probably remember from your last fight with one of us, we women are detail-oriented little devils who read volumes of meaning into even the most offhand things. To give you a taste of what we mean, we went to a bar, found a table of hotties who bore a striking resemblance to those tasty brunettes on the WB's Charmed, *and sent in a team of interns to eavesdrop on their evaluations of the hopeful guys who were checking them out. Some of their comments:*

"Baseball hat on backward. That's a thumbs-down because he probably doesn't know how to do his own laundry and watches sports on TV all day."

"Look, look, he's carrying The New Yorker *— he reads, he's smart, he cares about things! Oh, but wait, check out his glasses: He might be kind of a cold fish in bed."*

"Why does he have so much gel in his hair? Maybe he just got out of the shower because he goes running every day after work. No, no, it looks crunchy...I think he's a gel head. That's a no-go."

The way girls analyze guys' vital stats would put the dorkiest fantasy baseball commissioner to shame. But now that you know you're being watched, you can gain a distinct advantage over your blissfully oblivious competition. The advice in this chapter is designed to help you sail through her Sherlock Holmes–like investigation and come out smelling like a rose. You'll have her playing Lap Dance II: The Home Game *in no time.*

The Four Things All Women Want

"All women are looking for the same basic qualities in men," says Helen Fisher, author of *Anatomy of Love: The Mysteries of Mating, Marriage and Why We Stray* (Fawcett Books, 1995) and *First Sex: The Natural Talents of Women and How They Are Changing the World* (Random House, 1999). And she's got the statistics to prove it: In a study of 37 societies, Fisher found that while women do have their types, the same small handful of primal physical and mental characteristics lie at the heart of all women's guy wish lists. To subtly demonstrate that you'd fulfill all her subconscious needs, just show her you have...

1. Demonstrable resources

She doesn't need to know that your checks bounce like a romper room at snack time—here are some cheap tips to exaggerate your wealth, even from across a crowded room.

First, carry a money clip instead of a wallet. "It's an accessory that shows women you are financially secure enough to throw around the bills," says Karen, 34, a New York City–based fashion stylist and hot babe. (Bonus: Your ass will look less lumpy, too.) Next, whatever else you have to skimp on, drop some dough on the shoes.

Chicks gauge other women's fiscal health by looking at their shoes (it's generally easier to look good in inexpensive clothes than inexpensive shoes), and they'll judge you the same way. Shoes that look pricier usually are made of smooth, supple leather that doesn't crack over time, and thicker, more substantial soles.

Fisher also notes that a woman's subconscious attraction toward your "resources" includes your education. Since studies show that women are least confident in the subjects of math and science, displaying confidence here will convince her you're Einstein across the board. So bone up on The Learning Channel, and maybe when she passes you on the way to the powder room the snippet she'll hear will sound like, "Although it lives in the sea, the horseshoe crab can actually drown if you turn it upside down and pour water over it." If a fake Mensa card "accidentally" drops out of your wallet at the bar, that probably won't hurt either.

2. Status in the community

Since you can no longer run for public office—young interns are so bad at keeping secrets—at least make sure she knows you have a loyal constituency. Conveniently, this can consist of your drinking buddies or even the cashier at the bookstore. Explains Suzanne Lopez, author of *Get Smart With Your Heart* (Putnam, 1999), "Women are more likely to want to get to know you if they can see that other people enjoy your company and trust you."

Any connection with other people will help her forget the possibility that you're a crazed loner. If your friends are nowhere to be found when a surprisingly toasty Miss Norway walks in the door at Starbucks, strike up a quick bit of smiling chitchat with the cashier. "I met my boyfriend at a small club after spotting him talking to the band when they came offstage," says Julie, 30, a personal trainer in Minneapolis. "It turns out he didn't even know them, but the fact that he was where the action was made me want to be with him."

3. Physical prowess

Specifically, the studies Fisher cites actually show that women want men who are tall and have a strong jaw, but the overall implication is pretty clear. Her attitude is still biologically rooted in the days when women depended upon men to bring home the bacon in the form of a wild boar on a spear. "The modern man may lift no more than a pencil or a PowerBook, but good-looking men are still described in terms emphasizing size," says Nancy Etcoff, Ph.D., in her book *Survival of the Prettiest: The Science of Beauty* (Doubleday, 1999). Essentially, what her desire for someone tall and strong-jawed really means is that she wants to know that you, like Harrison Ford, can take care of her and protect her from wildebeests and strangers walking into the rest room while she's peeing.

The latter is what attracted Theresa, 23, a graduate student in Iowa City, Iowa, to a less-than-buff perfect stranger. "My girlfriend warned me that the lock was broken on the ladies' room but said the cute guy at the booth right next to it was letting people know when it was occupied. I went right over to check him out, because I like a guy who's into serving and protecting." Bottom line: Regardless of muscle tone, always play the part of the confident protector.

4. Emotional availability

Women say they're looking for a man who's "emotionally available." That's chick-speak for wanting a guy who'll listen to her prattle on about her issues with Mom and "that bitch at work who listens to my phone conversations." In Chapter 7 you'll learn how to deal with this issue in a real, how-did-I-get-myself-into-this relationship, but for now all you need to know is how to convince her you're patient and sensitive, willing to invest the time and effort to decode how she really feels out of whatever she feels compelled to say. How do you do this from a distance?

First, don't make the mistake of gazing over at her when your friend is talking to you. Sure, it seems like flattery that she's so gorgeous you can't possibly concentrate on the conversation at hand, but to her it signals that when she's the one chatting away, you'll be a million miles away mentally. Second, nod pensively as whomever you're talking to is speaking, even if he's just comparing tequila brands. Just change the conversation to the sad plight of the poor agave worms by the time she saunters over to within earshot.

WHAT REELS US IN?

We asked women nationwide which first impressions make their heads spin faster than Linda Blair's (in a good way). The key seems to be self-restraint: All things in moderation. Here's the thumbnail guide to making a beautiful stranger intrigued enough to keep listening.

BE FUNNY... "He has to crack me up on a regular basis. I'll forgive a lot if he makes me laugh." —Donna, 29, social worker, San Francisco

...but don't try too hard. "Guys who are always trying to be the center of attention get to be so exhausting. You don't have to put on a 24-hour puppet show to impress me. I can be pretty damn entertaining myself." —Pepper, 27, waitress, Baltimore

BE AMBITIOUS... "A guy in a suit and tie is such a turn-on. How could I feel excited about going to bed with some boy whose biggest long-term goal is to see how many nights in a row he can drink until 5:00 a.m. and still drag himself into his dead-end job the next day?" —Marcy, 25, account executive, Portland, Maine

...but not obsessed with work. "I don't want the guy who works 24 hours a day—how's he going to have any time for me? I want a guy who has an adventuresome spirit, who's interested in the rest of the world. If he doesn't have that, it doesn't matter how rich, smart, or good-looking he is." —Sara, 26, writer, San Francisco

The 10 Clothing Rules
Women Wish You Knew

1. Shoes and socks should match.
Dark dress shoes call for dark dress socks—save the white tube socks with the red stripes for your sneakers. Never, ever wear black socks with light-colored shoes.

2. Belt width matters.
Wear a narrower belt for dressy wear (i.e., suit, jacket, and tie); wear a wider belt with jeans or khakis and a T-shirt. Also, belt color should match shoe color.

3. Shirts should almost always be tucked in.
The biggest exception: when you're wearing swim trunks, drawstring shorts, or cut-off jeans at the beach. Or when you're not wearing pants at all.

4. Clogs and sandals with narrow straps are for sissies.
Stick to athletic-type sandals, like Tevas or cheapo dime-store flip-flops.

5. Never wear ties with short-sleeved button-downs.
Remember Ernie on *My Three Sons*? Not a good look. Wear short-sleeve button-downs untucked and unbuttoned over a T-shirt...or not at all.

6. If you're not sure your shirt and pants go together, they don't.
A no-fail plan: Choose a colored item—shirt or pants—then pick a solid neutral (tan, gray, black, white) to go with it. You'll never go wrong with this trick, and she'll think you're more than all right.

7. Suits should be worn for job interviews, indoor weddings, and funerals. And that's it.
Wearing a suit on a date when you haven't just come from work will scare almost

BE CONFIDENT... "The most important thing is self-confidence. Not cockiness, but he should be self-assured enough that you don't have to worry about hurting his feelings when you're joking around." —Rachel, 29, writer, New York City
...but not conceited. "There's nothing worse than arrogance. If a guy acts like he's superior to everyone else, you know he's not going to be good in bed—he'll be too self-involved to care about getting you off." —Amber, 24, lawyer, Manchester, New Hampshire

BE ATTENTIVE... "I like to be worshiped a little. You know, compliments and lots of gazing in my eyes. Who wouldn't?" —Beth, 21, property management assistant, Des Moines, Iowa
...but not smothering. "If a man worships you 24-7, it's hard to respect him. He stops being a manly man and becomes a puppy dog cowering at your feet." —Rebecca, 22, student, Austin, Texas

BE INTELLIGENT... "He has to be smart—that makes up for almost anything." —Katherine, 24, copy editor, Atlanta
...but not stuffy. "Don't be too reserved. I love it when guys will embarrass themselves—or me—in public for the sake of humor." —Helen, 28, cooking student, New York City

BE SECURE IN YOURSELF... "I like a guy who's smart and successful but who doesn't have to prove it to anyone." —Trina, 27, musician, Alameida, California
...but not without goals. "My boyfriend likes to talk about his future plans—cool vacations, new job opportunities—and I like that he's always thinking about how to make life better." —Michele, 31, researcher, Princeton, New Jersey

any woman. Khakis and a jacket will handle going out to dinner, informal shotgun weddings, and church.

8. Avoid pattern-to-pattern combos.
Don't mix plaid shirts with striped pants, paisley with checks, etc.—no straight man can pull this off. Also, plaid is for shirts, not pants—leave your grandpa's closet alone.

9. Bow ties are high-risk, low-payoff.
Stick with the traditional tie for that first formal impression. If you're nuts about bow ties, at least ask her what she thinks of them before allying yourself with former senator Paul Simon and Pee-wee Herman.

10. Blue never fails.
Few men look bad in blue—it's a versatile color that can work at a formal or casual place. Most women agree there's nothing sexier than a guy in a blue button-down.

Look Dressed...Not Obsessed

Ten out of ten women agree: You should look like you paid attention to what you're wearing, but not like you changed three times to achieve the perfect ensemble. (*We'll* handle that, thank you.) "Being *too* put together, working too hard is always a cause for alarm," says Kim Johnson Gross, author of *Chic Simple Women's Wardrobe* (Knopf, 1995). To her, fashion-plate perfection will signal you're either gay, a control freak, or—yikes!—German.

DRESS FOR SEX-CESS!

Shirts
Never wear: Tank tops (especially "wife beaters," which scare women). Short-sleeved button-downs with a tie, à la *My Three Sons.* Day-Glo colors. Non-cow-colored leather. Bill Cosby–esque patterned sweaters. Anything mesh, too tight, unbuttoned to the waist, or spandex. (Spandex is considered a sure sign you *really* like show tunes and decorating.)

Instead, try: T-shirts that fit (that means the sleeve seam is on or close to the end of your shoulder). Button-down shirts without a tie. Solid-color sweaters (they show you're a solid guy). Black or brown leather jackets. "I've been attracted to some ugly-shirt-wearing guys in my time—a terry-cloth orange-and-yellow paisley comes to mind—but the attraction was in spite of these shirts, not because of them," says Liz, 29, an urban planner in Pitts-

Why go to the trouble of exploring clothing beyond jeans and a rope belt? Because it's an easy way to leapfrog over your competition: Since most guys are too lazy to learn the basics that separate the savages from the civilized, just dressing adequately puts you way ahead of the game. Here's our item-by-item guide to fashion choices that'll make her want to rip all your clothes off.

burgh. "I like a guy in a button-down shirt, but what will really get me is a good solid-color sweater, maybe a V-neck, with a T-shirt underneath it."

Pants/Shorts
Never wear: Too tight anything, too baggy anything, acid-washed jeans, parachute pants, denim shorts that aren't cutoffs. "Men should never wear those Joey Buttafuoco pants," says Kate, 28, a teacher in Chicago.

Instead, try: Clean, newish denim is the big winner here, followed by khakis. "A good pair of blue denim Levi's never goes out of style," explains Cheryl, 23, a wedding planner in Charleston, South Carolina. "This may sound terrible, but I really like a guy's butt in a pair of Levi's... assuming it's a good butt."

Underwear
Never wear: Bikini briefs, a.k.a. banana hammocks. There must be some woman out there who likes

"I like it when it looks like a guy just picked his clothes up off the floor and came up with something good: a cool T-shirt, for example, or colorful sneakers. Guys should never look like they thought for more than two minutes about their outfits." —Hannah, 24, model, New York City

"A guy shouldn't be afraid to take chances with clothes. It shows he's comfortable with himself and has a sense of humor. Orange socks, a bright winter scarf. Not a clown outfit—just well accented." —Fiona, 30, musician, Los Angeles

"I like to see an outfit that isn't necessarily an ensemble you'd buy together at a store, but something that is hip and cool and pieced together to really say who he is." —Grace, 27, waitress, Philadelphia

"A neat appearance that doesn't look like he's trying too hard—definitely no designer names plastered across his chest." —Lorna, 24, accountant, Santa Barbara, California

"Guys should wear clothes that fit them properly and are flattering to their particular physiques. Too much flesh exposed is always a big no-no—I don't care how great his body is." —Priscilla, 30, bonds analyst, Chicago

"I tend to go for the casual look. Uptight makes me run the other way, so I'd prefer a colored T-shirt with khakis instead of a button-down shirt. Ties are for work and weddings." —Rebecca, 22, student, Austin, Texas

them, but everyone we polled gave them the thumbs-down.

Instead, try: Boxer shorts or briefs that fit and don't have nasty holes or stains. According to Greta, 25, a theater manager in Madison, Wisconsin. "Every guy should wear boxers. There's just nothing that appealing about seeing his package all squished up inside tighty-whiteys."

Swim Trunks
Never wear: Speedos. Unless you're an Olympic swimmer (no, no—a *real* Olympic swimmer). There isn't a woman in America who thinks a Speedo looks good on you.

Instead, try: Trunks. The hem should come down halfway between your crotch and your knee. If your legs are superskinny, consider those jam-style trunks with the hem that hits you at the knee. "When I first met my boyfriend," says Sara, 26, a writer in San Francisco, "he was wearing long surf trunks and nothing else. As much as I hate to sound shallow, both the suit and the body got my full and rapt attention."

Shoes
Never wear: Euro-type sandals (the kind that make you unsure whether you're in the women's or the men's section), especially open-toed ones. White sweat socks with black shoes (or dress socks with sneakers).

Instead, try: Shoes and socks that match the occasion: quality dress shoes with dark socks for work; nonratty sneakers or casual shoes with white socks for play. "If a guy's going to wear dress shoes, they shouldn't be too businesslike," advises Wendy, 30, a musician in New York City. "Tassels are a big turn-off, but give me a good pair of lace-up wingtips any day."

Accessories
Never wear: Jewelry of any kind, especially earrings, necklaces, or flashy gold pieces. (Unless it's a wedding ring, in which case maybe, just maybe, you shouldn't be quite so concerned about picking up women.) "A gold chain or dangling earring can sabotage an otherwise good-looking guy," says Nora, 27, a financial analyst in Kansas City, Missouri.

Instead, try: A nice watch. Still the only universally accepted bit of male jewelry. It says you've got money *and* won't be late for your hot date.

For Fashion Imbeciles Only:
The Best Chick Date Ever

Got black, acid-washed jeans? Tiny alligators on your shirts? Anything in terry cloth? Maybe you've been so busy raking in the dough, waxing your muscle car, or perfecting your PlayStation technique that you haven't overhauled your wardrobe since 1982. Never fear: We're going to help you upgrade your closet into a babe-magnetic paradise *and* make some lucky girl insanely happy in the bargain. The trick: Take a woman shopping with you—other than your mom.

Why would a free woman ever agree to share this dismal chore? Because we're genetically predisposed to think it's fun—very few women will ever turn down an opportunity to shop, particularly for clothes and particularly in the role of expert consultant. "I've given quite a few guys style makeovers in the past—it's part of our duty as women," says Kathleen, 30, an engineer in Providence.

This is key, according to fashion expert Gross: "Make sure you go with a woman who knows you well, or you'll end up with clothes that never leave your closet." Stick with your own instincts, but use her to help give you an overall idea of what you need more of in your wardrobe. "If you usually dress very classic or tailored and you want to try a more casual look, tell her so she can help you decide whether you look hip and relaxed or just shapeless and slumpy," says Gross. The dark side of this strategy: It can't be used on a woman

---

SOLE SEARCHING:

When she's not looking, you're checking out her chest; when you're not looking, she's checking out your shoes. So make sure your feet are telling her what you want them to say—it's easy to turn a girl off with an unintentionally inconsistent message. "It's weird when a guy seems alternative and hipsterlike but is wearing shiny loafers with tassels—it's like he doesn't know who he is," says Justine, 24, a loan officer in Tampa. How your heels make them feel:

Shoe: Orange Converse high tops
She thinks: You're fun-loving, you don't have a job that involves a tie, and you'll play pretend games with her three-year-old niece.

Shoe: Black wingtips
She thinks: You're an old-school traditionalist, and you'll rent black-and-white movies with her.

Shoe: Brown suede bucks
She thinks: You're also a fan of corduroy pants and like to cuddle in front of the fire.

Shoe: Loafers with tassels
She thinks: You're old money, so you don't feel the need to worry about fashion.

you're interested in dating—your clothes are only impressive if she thinks you chose them all by yourself, champ.

Grooming Made Easy

Why should you go to all the trouble to look fresh and spend more than $9.99 on a haircut? Because it's these little tweaks that'll get you called up from minor-league dating to the big show. According to the 1995 survey *Sex in America,* compiled by the National Opinion Research Center at the University of Chicago, couples are usually equivalently matched in the looks depart-ment. "In other words, the better one looks, the better-looking one's partner is likely to be," explains Nancy Etcoff in *Survival of the Prettiest.* So now you know.

Get the Edge
With a Perfect Shave

You don't need shaving tips—you've been shaving for years, right? Yes...but your standards are dismally low. "Most guys rush through the shave just to get it over with, but protecting the skin and really going after each hair is worth the extra time," says Eric Malka, co-owner of The Art of Shaving, a full-service barbershop and boutique in New York City. Here's why that extra-close shave's worth the bother: Because we women have smooth, baby-soft faces and vulnerable inner thighs (heh, heh) that get ravaged by your half-assed quickie efforts. We're *mucho* impressed by a close, smooth shave because we know you didn't do it for yourself—you did it for us.

WHAT YOUR SHOES TELL HER ABOUT YOU

Shoe: Plain black lace-ups
She thinks: It depends. With a substantial sole (thick but not platform), she thinks you're a stand-up, good guy. With skinny, weak soles, she thinks you wish you someday could be a tap-dancer.

Shoe: Black leather or suede slip-ons with buckles
She thinks: You're Eurotrashy and will be rude to waiters.

Shoe: Retro suede sneakers
She thinks: You have some clue about style and trends, since this shoe goes beyond just the 'work shoe' and 'workout shoe' basics. Artsy gals will love it; traditional gals may find it too whimsical.

Shoe: Shit-kicker boots with square, steel-reinforced toes
She thinks: You're either rugged and outdoorsy or love edgy music—she'll check your haircut to see which one. If she can't see your haircut because of the 10-gallon hat, she'll know you're planning to drink heavily and start a bar brawl.

Shoe: Running shoes
She thinks: If you're not actually running, it says you choose comfort over fashion and probably have a reliable car, but it also sends an "I'm not very style conscious" message, too. Expect mixed results.

The work-intensive method that follows can double or triple your shave time, but here's how to justify it. When you have a date or know you'll be bumping into babes, go on and execute this perfect shave; skip shaving altogether on days you're unlikely to come into close contact with chafeable ladies. Bonus: You'll get a closer shave when you need it. "It will be easier to get closer with less irritation, because there's more hair to shave," Malka says.

So here's the technique. Before you shave, soften the hair as much as possible by taking a hot shower; then apply a preshave oil to lubricate your skin and protect it from the razor. Use hot water and a lubricating shaving cream or shaving soap; Malka advises finding one that contains aloe or lanolin, such as Kiss My Face Fragrance Free Moisture Shave, Clinique M Shave Aloe Gel, or Noxzema Shave with Aloe and Lanolin.

You're going to shave in three different directions, making sure you always have a protective layer of shaving cream between the razor and your skin. First, go straight down from the top of the cheek to the bottom of the neck, including the mustache area, using almost no pressure on the razor. Rinse your face with hot water, and then lather up again. This time, go from the bottom of the neck to the top of the cheek. Rinse and relather, then shave sideways, going from the outside in. "Going across the grain like this will grab the hairs that grow in different directions," Malka says.

When you're finished, apply cold water to your skin and use a moisturizing aftershave or balm. Skip astringents and alcohol-based aftershaves, which will dry out your skin. Dry off your face. Smile.

Do You Stink?
How to guarantee you'll always smell like a man she wants to get closer to

Flashback: 1985. Few people know this, but that was the year the world narrowly avoided widespread chemical-warfare-style asphyxiation. The culprit? No, not the Ayatollah, but the millions of *Miami Vice* disciples who copied Don Johnson's sockless look. Had they all simultaneously removed their shoes on any humid day that summer, the earth would have been strangled by foot foulness of a most toxic variety. And at the very moment of the mass suffocation of humankind, the pastel-clad killers would've all gasped the same last words: "I...don't...smell...anything...bad."

That's the cruel irony of bad breath and body odor: The worst offenders have no idea how offensive they are. "The smell comes on so gradually that they just get used to it," says Alan Hirsch, M.D., director of the Smell & Taste Treatment and Research Foundation in Chicago. Unfortunately, the classic blow-into-your-hands and the crude scratch-and-sniff-your-ass techniques for detecting

WHEN SHE'S NOT LOOKING, YOU'RE CHECKING OUT HER CHEST; WHEN YOU'RE NOT LOOKING, SHE'S CHECKING OUT YOUR SHOES.

You know she has a weakness for shopping—you can use this to your evil advantage. Paco Underhill, author of *Why We Buy: The Science of Shopping* (Simon & Schuster, 1999), has spent more than 20 years studying the finer points of what turns browsers into buyers. Manipulate her decision making with these inside tips and she'll never know you tricked her into carting you home.

Shopping wisdom: People need a transition zone when they enter a store—any attempt to sell to them within the first 10 feet will be useless.	**How to take advantage:** Don't pounce on a good-looking woman the second she enters the room, or you'll just make her uncomfortable; give her time to adjust and scope out the scene.
Shopping wisdom: People slow down when they see reflective surfaces.	**How to take advantage:** If there's a mirror behind the bar, park yourself on a bar stool. If not, try to find a mirror, and park yourself at the nearest table. You're more likely to catch her attention and pique her interest.
Shopping wisdom: When people enter a store, they always walk toward the right, and they tend not to walk all the way through a store aisle; once they've found what they want, they turn around.	**How to take advantage:** Set up your position on the right side of the room when you get a choice—play your cards right and she'll never make it around to the guys on the left.
Shopping wisdom: Women hate being jostled from the rear while shopping—the dreaded "butt brush."	**How to take advantage:** If you're talking to a woman, lead her out of the path of traffic so she's not being bumped by people walking by. She's less likely to become annoyed and walk away (plus, you get to play her protector—a double whammy).
Shopping wisdom: In fast-food restaurants, women tend to choose more private tables in the rear.	**How to take advantage:** Women don't really want to be on public display while scarfing down a Big Mac. So consider the location: In high-end bars, they'll ostentiously hang out near the picture windows at the front. So position yourself accordingly.

stink don't work. So if you have an infamously malodorous friend, it's absolutely your duty to clue him in. And if someone is ballsy enough to tell you that you've got B.O., for God's sake, don't get P.O.'d—get clean.

Foulness #1: Putrid pits

Here's a bit of B.O. trivia that will amaze your buds: Sweat doesn't stink. "The billions of harmless bacteria that live on everyone's skin are the real culprits," says Dr. Hirsch. "When the microbes mix with perspiration, body odor is produced." And the more time bacteria have to blend with perspiration, the stinkier you get. This explains why you're not rank immediately after a sweaty run, but if you hang out without showering or changing, you start to ripen.

Certain body parts definitely have more smell potential than others, though.

SEDUCE HER WITH YOUR SCENT

Women use all five senses when they're deciding whether you're worthy, so don't neglect her sense of smell. What is your cologne telling women about you even before you open your mouth? Here, Linda Zielke, counter manager for men's and women's fragrances at Saks Fifth Avenue in Short Hills, New Jersey, explains what your cologne is saying to your gal.

Type: Citrusy
Examples: cK by Calvin Klein, Paco by Paco Rabanne, Tuscany by Aramis
What it says to her: You'll surprise her with a weekend getaway, and you'll get along with her dad.

Type: Woodsy
Examples: Safari for Men by Ralph Lauren, Polo by Ralph Lauren, Havana by Aramis
What it says to her: You know your way around a chainsaw and will open the door for her.

Type: Sweet
Examples: Obsession for Men by Calvin Klein, By from Dolce & Gabbana,
Le Male by Jean Paul Gaultier
What it says to her: You'll insist on paying for dinner and give her an amazing massage later.

Type: Spicy
Examples: Classic Escada by Escada, Bellami by Hermès, Emporio Armani by Emporio Armani
What it says to her: You'll take her dancing, and you prefer wine to beer.

Type: None
What it says to her: You're confident that you smell great without any cologne. (So make sure you do by using a deodorant soap and avoiding spicy foods, particularly curry and garlic spices, which stick around for a long time.)

Still not sure which one sounds like you? If in doubt, stick with that first one. "The most popular fragrances for men of all ages are probably those that are citrusy," says Zielke. "Citrusy fragrances are very clean, light, and classic." Just like you, right?

Armpits are the site of not only sweat glands but also apocrine glands, which release a high-density steroid that scientists believe may influence sexual behavior. When this steroid mixes and mingles with bacteria—which thrive in the moist warmth of those recesses—it produces an oily odor. And since more perspiration means more chance of bacteria-fueled fumes, if you sweat like a rain forest, the following advice goes double for you.

Bacteria build up when you don't bathe, so here's a no-brainer first step: Take a shower. Blitz bacterial nasties by lathering up with an antibacterial soap containing Triclosan or ethyl alcohol, such as Purell or Softsoap. Both have gender-neutral scents that won't make you smell like potpourri.

After showering, dust yourself with talc to keep your skin dry. (Booty-getting bonus tip: In a recent study of scents and sexual arousal, baby powder turned out to be a major turn-on for women.) Then underarm yourself properly. Antiperspirants contain aluminum salts, which temporarily plug sweat ducts. Deodorants contain bacteria-blasting ingredients such as Triclosan, as well as fragrances that mask odor. Thus, the antiperspirant-deodorant combo is a B.O.-slamming double whammy.

Finally, wear shirts with built-in breathability—cotton and linen are classic standbys—with cotton undershirts. "Cotton wicks perspiration away from your body," explains Gray Maycumber, who reports on fibers and fabrics as a senior editor at *DNR,* a trade magazine for the men's apparel industry. Bacteria then have less of an opportunity to mix with your sweat. Acrylic, nylon, and polyester shirts and sweaters, on the other hand, hold perspiration against your body.

And look for a new fabric called CoolMax, developed specifically for "moisture management." It was first used in activewear but is making its way into other clothes. Check for it on clothing labels.

Foulness #2: Foot funk

"Chee-toes" and other foul foot odors are also caused by a familiar combo: bacteria and sweat. "Shoes are a perfect incubator. They make your feet hot and sweaty, which increases the number of odor-causing bacteria," says Michael L. Ramsey, M.D., an associate in the department of dermatology at Penn State Geisinger Medical Center in Danville, Pennsylvania.

Charcoal shoe inserts and foot powders cover up the smell but won't stop it at its source. If your idea of washing your feet is letting the sudsy water hit them as you rinse the shampoo out of your hair, you need serious shower rehab. Try scrubbing your feet with antibacterial soap, especially between the toes. After rinsing, dry your dogs thoroughly. (A blow-dryer is effective.) "You can also spray your feet with an underarm antiperspirant," says Dr. Ramsey, who wrote an article for the journal *The Physician and Sportsmedicine* entitled "Foot Odor: How to Clear the Air."

THE CRUEL IRONY OF BAD BREATH AND BAD BODY ODOR: THE WORST OFFENDERS HAVE NO IDEA HOW OFFENSIVE THEY ARE.

Choose footwear carefully. "Leather is a good choice, because it's porous," he says. "Skip synthetic uppers"—the part that's not the sole. And make sure they fit: Your feet can't breathe in shoes that are too tight. If you go sockless—sandals being the exception—you're begging for a big-time stank fest. "Cotton socks are crucial for absorbing sweat," says Dr. Ramsey. And if you have a real foot-odor problem, change your socks at least twice during the day. Sneakers with a noticeably noxious bouquet can be scrubbed clean with detergent and bleach, either by hand or in a washing machine on the hot-water cycle, then allowed to air-dry. If your dress shoes stink, however, chuck them.

If you've tried all of the above for two to three weeks and the odor is still kicking, see an M.D., because you may have athlete's foot, the classic fungus that thrives in the warm, moist areas between the toes. Or it could be pitted keratolysis, a condition caused by li'l bacterial bastards that dig tiny pits in the bottoms of your feet. In either case, a doctor can prescribe a topical antifungal or antibacterial cream.

Foulness #3:
Hellacious Halitosis

Your first priority is to find out whether you are indeed violating others' human rights just by breathing. "Asking your spouse or a close friend is the best method of at-home breath testing," says Martin Rotman, D.D.S., a dentist in Beverly Hills, California. Alternatively, try the "spoon test" recommended by the California Dental Association: Scrape the crud off the back of your tongue with a disposable plastic spoon, then take a whiff. If it stinks, chances are your breath does, too.

Why does this test work? Of the more than 200 types of bacteria that call your mouth home, the main culprits for halitosis are the sulfur-producing varieties that hang out at the back of the tongue. "Your tongue should be pink. Any white coating is plaque and debris, which contribute to bad breath," says Dr. Rotman.

Drugstores sell plastic tongue scrapers to remedy the problem, but, Dr. Rotman says, a toothbrush works just as well.

Dry mouth is also a major contributor to garbage breath, since saliva enhances the mouth's natural ability to clean itself. Eating small meals often, drinking water, chewing gum, and sucking on candy all restock your spit. But guess what: Mouthwash makes things worse. "Many mouthwashes have alcohol in them, which dries out the mouth and ultimately generates more foul-smelling bacteria," Dr. Rotman says.

And if you love spicy foods, like garlic and onions, all the brushing in the world won't help. "When these foods are broken down, the by-products enter the bloodstream and are exhaled when you breathe, for four to six hours or longer," explains Dr. Rotman. You don't have to give up your stinky favorites, though. Dr. Rotman says taking two or three capsules of BreathAsure, available at drugstores, immediately after eating prevents those by-products from getting into your bloodstream. Your kissable breath should last four to six hours, or until you eat again.

Still making bystanders weep? Decaying teeth or periodontal disease may be upping the muck factor in your mouth. Drag your butt to the dentist: Sparkling choppers aren't attractive just because they look good. A pearly smile signals kissable breath.

Look Fitter
Without Working Out

You could try to look like a muscle-bound mammoth who lives at the gym, but why bother, since most women say that's not what they want? "Sure I want a man who looks fit, but if he's beyond buff, with rock-hard pecs, I'd worry that he spends all of his time at the gym—and that he won't have time for me," says Giselle, 22, an administrative assistant in New York City. Here, Neil Maki, a fitness instructor and a spokesman for the American Council on Exercise, gives you tips on how to look fitter instantly.

First, remember how Ma nagged you to stand up straighter? She was right. Standing with your shoulders thrown back and down, your butt slightly tucked in (which makes your gut look flatter), and your head held high will make you look taller, trimmer, and more confident. "It's amazing how many guys work so hard on their bodies and then forget this finishing touch," says Maki. "If you stand tall, no matter what you look like, you'll look confident and like you have your act together."

Next, if you know you may be bumping into potential pretty playmates, avoid certain foods that day and the day before, because what you put in your mouth can affect your appearance. For example, stay away from processed foods. "Keep away from fast food and things that are frozen, canned, or boxed," says Maki. "Most of them are very high in

SEX IS IN THE AIR

Do your natural emissions make the difference between love at first sight and another lonely night?

Anyone who has observed dogs' intricate, crotch-nuzzling mating rituals (and let's hope you don't make frequent efforts to do this) knows that scent has a big-time effect on animals' sexual behavior. So do other, unscented chemicals that are picked up via the vomeronasal organ (VNO), a sensory structure in the nose that is separate from the sense of smell.

In the early '90s, scientists at the University of Utah discovered that the VNO in humans picks up chemical messengers called pheromones. The pheromone released by men actually has a calming effect on the fairer, more neurotic sex. So while pheromones aren't the aphrodisiacs that perfume sellers make them out to be, they do mellow women out a bit. And if you've ever tried to get amorous with a stressed-out woman, you know this is a major plus.

sodium, which will make you retain water and look bloated."

Some easy long-term advice: In general, when you're eating out, have an extra glass of water instead of an appetizer, and always leave something on your plate. That extra course or supersize portion can mean up to 300 extra calories per meal, and every 10 of those can add up to a pound. The extra glasses of water (ideally, you should be drinking eight a day) will also make your skin look fresher and clearer.

Finally, don't fall into the trap of thinking that doing 100 killer crunches to flatten your stomach—or other spot-workout tricks—will help you quickly look leaner and keener. "Targeting a specific area, like the beer gut, won't give you quick results," says Maki. Your best bet is to get regular cardiovascular exercise, ideally 30 minutes three to five times a week, to make any fat disappear and your abs reappear.

chapter two

Score That First Date

Now that you've got her interested, here's how to get her involved. You've targeted a tasty little treat from across a crowded bar or Laundromat or AA meeting, and you used the information in the last chapter to catch her eye and maybe even get her talking. She's smart, funny, beautiful...and way out of what used to be your league. So how are you supposed to connive her into agreeing to go out with a schmo like you?

"That first conversation is incredibly important to women," says Lillian Glass, Ph.D., psychologist and author of He Says She Says: Closing the Communication Gap Between the Sexes (Perigee, 1984). "She's looking for sincerity, and for you to make her comfortable. Just get her talking—and listen—and you'll put her at ease."

It's easy to assume she'll be turned off by a guy who waltzes up and lays a line on her, but the women we talked to say that isn't true. When it comes to the modern mating dance, they enjoy being passive and want you to be aggressive. "When a guy approaches me like he's interested, it's an automatic compliment," says Janelle, 28, a sales representative in Omaha. "He saw something he liked, so unless he's a total freak, I'm going to feel pleased enough to at least hear what he has to say."

What you say still matters, of course. Stay away from snore-inducing cheesy lines ("Am I in heaven? Because I'm looking at an angel"). Instead, try complimenting something she's wearing—our gals said this works because you're really complimenting her taste, which is high praise in the chick world.

For more pick-up tricks girls wouldn't reveal until now, read on: These surefire suggestions should help you reel her in before she has time to realize the horrible, horrible mistake she's about to make. We can't guarantee Heidi Klum will agree to hit that nude beach with you, but we promise to give you your best possible shot.

Five Conversations
She's Always Happy to Have

It's a simple equation: The sooner you get a dialogue going full throttle, the quicker you get to see nipple. But going through the agonizing "So what do you do?" and "Have I seen you here before?" is the conversation-sparking equivalent of soggy matches. Instead, turn up the flame with these chick-conversation starters—and stop making her wait so long for the meat.

Conversation starter #1:
"Where did you get your shoes/interesting ring/haircut?"

Women's favorite shoptalk is, no pun intended, shopping. Stay away from the majors—pants, skirts, shirts, etc.—or she might think you're gay, but hit an interesting accessory, something she obviously added specifically to catch eyes, and her

TOP 10 BLATHERINGS
THAT WILL MAKE HER TURN AND RUN

Sure, you know not to spout these nookie-damning knuckleheadisms—just rip out this page and give it to your most pathetic buddy. If you want to keep her talking, never ever ever...

...Pun on her name. For example, "Your name is Sandy? As in hot, gorgeous sandy beaches, oh yeah!" A scarlet "L" has just appeared on your chest.

...Pick a fight with a guy who bumps into her. It seemed macho and cute on the playground in elementary school, but all she'll think now is, *I bet this guy has a gun! Oooh, gross!*

...Mouth lyrics along with the song that's playing. The verbal equivalent of playing air guitar, this move says, "I'm the man from your worst karaoke nightmares." It's a typical barroom jukebox—of course you know the lyrics.

...Use the word *baby*. Unless you're a legitimate Hollywood director, this is out—you might as well drive up with a

"Pedophiles R Us" bumper sticker.

...Tell her she looks like Gwyneth. Or Winona, or Drew, etc. A woman's entire life is one big internal comparathon with other chicks. Sure, you mean well, but this line will just make her think about how Tyra's breasts are perkier than hers. You lose.

...Go all freaky poetic and tell her how you felt (awestruck, filled with déjà vu, inspired) when you first spotted her just before. The first impression is the one and only time when a woman *doesn't* want to know how you feel. Why? Because she's still trying to determine if you're this summer's Son of Sam.

...Ask her, "What's a nice girl..." You know the rest. Cars

with fins may have come back into style, but this line needs to find a cushy coffin, RIP circa 1955.

...Open up with a quote she's supposed to be able to reference, whether it's Shakespeare or the Goo Goo Dolls. Don't test the merchandise: Even if you luck out with a gal who loves *Jeopardy!*, odds are she won't want to do the wild thing with Alex Trebek.

...Ask, "Can I borrow a quarter?" It seems like a good way to lure her to the jukebox or segue into a sweet conversation about how you have to call and check on your dear geriatric relative, right? Wrong. To her, your simple request says: "I cannot provide for you. You are just a handbag with legs."

own will light up. For 20 minutes after you show interest, she'll prattle on about sales, styles, trends, and how she's a weird size because of X, Y, and Z. (You're even allowed to surreptitiously check out her bod at this point—just make sure to say, "Well, you look great to me!")

Conversation starter #2:
"What was the best vacation you've ever taken?"
The nonthreatening subject matter lets you sneak in under her radar—she'll go here even if she doesn't like you yet—and you'll conjure up happy thoughts and memories, which she'll then associate with you. She'll tell you everything from the thread count of the hotel sheets to how she wished she would have brought her blue bikini because it seemed like all the European women were wearing red ones. You just keep confirming that it sounds fantastic and pushing the happy-happy buttons. (If it was a foreign vacation, you're cleared to ask if she went topless—as long as you blush a little as you ask it—because American women always have an opinion on the when-in-Rome boob-baring issue.)

Conversation starter #3:
"Do you enjoy your work?"
The women we polled said they judge men by whether they ask about a girl's career (if not, it seems like he doesn't care about how she spends her days—only her nights). Asking her what she does and leaving it at that, however, is a guy's game: She'll feel judged by her success or lack of it. But how she feels about what she does? That's Woman Land, and a welcome conversation; she'll give you an earful whether she enjoys her job or not. If she loves her job and the conversation teeters, ask her if she's encountered a "glass ceiling"; that'll get her riled up and passionate. As a bonus, this strategy tells her you're sensitive and care about feelings. Psych!

Conversation starter #4:
"Do you get to see your family as often as you'd like?"
The answer's kind of irrelevant: She's bound to have some sort of "issues" with them, and she'll either want to talk about them or chat up a storm trying to avoid thinking about/talking about them. Plus, the opportunity to talk with an interest-ed guy about family issues is like cheese to a starving mouse. Finally, even if she has the perfect family, she's still likely to have guilt for not seeing them enough, which will put her in an emotionally vulnerable state. She'll be craving a big hug and maybe even—if you don't look too much like her brother—other affectionate activities.

Conversation starter #5:
"What's the big deal about Nicole Kidman/
Cameron Diaz/Julia Roberts?"
You aren't expressing an opinion here—and don't let her trick you into spilling

yours first—but you can bet she will, because women love to dish about stars, whether they worship or despise them. This question inevitably invites her to share her thesis on a female celebrity's style, acting ability, and breast authenticity. (That's right, she'll be talking about the shape and volume of other women's boobs!) Steer the conversation toward scandal and before you know it you're talking about sex.

Pick-up Tip of the Day: Neurolinguistic Programming

When chatting up women, try whenever possible to bring up positive memories that make her smiley and bright-eyed. Research shows that when you can get a gal talking about something happy from her past, she'll transfer those thrilled feelings onto you. "When she recalls something that made her feel good, she re-creates those feelings and begins to associate them with you," says Joan Irvine, a clinical hypnotherapist and coauthor of *Recipes for Hot Sex* (Lion's Head, 1998). The process is called neurolinguistic programming. Keep up the training and she'll start salivating every time you say "Remember…"

9 PHRASES TO THROW INTO THE CONVERSATION TO SHOW HER YOU'RE SHAG-WORTHY

Now that you're engaging in friendly chat with her, you may think you've won her over. Wrong again: The truth is, she's still reading you like a book, skimming your conversation for clues that you're worth the trouble of bikini waxing, lingerie donning, and all that. Here are some phrases to sprinkle in that will spoon-feed her into submission.

1. "…I think I was building bookshelves that weekend…"
What it says to her: You can build things *and* you read.

2. "…rates were so cheap in Indonesia/Nepal/Chile…"
What it says to her: You're brave *and* open to new experiences.

3. "…I'd flown back for my grandmother's 80th birthday…"
What it says to her: You'll make sacrifices for relationships *and* you won't blow off her birthday.

4. "…and we danced for hours…"
What it says to her: You don't have a problem with commitment *and* you're great in bed.

5. "…I'm thinking about running in the corporate half-marathon to raise money for AIDS/breast cancer/muscular dystrophy…"
What it says to her: You're fit *and* philanthropic.

6. "…but I didn't want to miss my flying lessons/race-car-driving lessons/yacht-racing lessons…"
What it says to her: You're a skilled adventurer *and* you'll be able to find her love button in the dark.

7. "…I remember always spending Christmas in a different country…"
What it says to her: Holidays are important to you *and* your family can provide a safety net so she'll never want for designer shoes.

8. "…almost finished that patent application…"
What it says to her: You're creative *and* motivated (so you'll probably plan a great honeymoon).

9. "…getting up at 6 a.m. to drive my little sister to camp…"
What it says to her: You're responsible *and* you'll always bring condoms.

Fine-Tune Your Approach

Women are usually happy to dish about mistakes guys have made while trying to pick them up, but they can be annoyingly loath to give up what does work for them—that would be like handing over the keys to the chastity belt. "That's like letting a guy read my diary," says Samantha, 28, a buyer at a department store in Philadelphia. Still, after plying Samantha and five of her most high-maintenance, ice-princess pals with fruity frozen drinks for two hours, we loosened up their lips. (Oh, stop—you know what we mean.) Here's a guide on the moves that charm even the most hard-to-crack-a-smile chicks.

Pretend your friend talked you into coming over. Yes, it's cheesy and proves you've been checking us out from afar, but it gives us an excuse to look directly at you guys, check you out, and then merge the two groups so there's no one-on-one pressure. Make sure to be smiling sweetly and laughing at your buddy when we look over. Also, stick with something lighthearted and goofy, like, "My friends bet me to come over here and ask you what's your sign/favorite drink/favorite MTV *Real World* cast." Explains Janice, 23, a nursing student in Dayton: "They looked so sheepish, we just laughed and invited them over. The guys offered to buy us a pitcher, and the really cute one made a beeline for the empty stool next to me. It was comfortable because we talked as a group the whole time, and then as we were leaving we exchanged numbers—and we've been dating for five months."

Move in super slow-mo. Lots of women, particularly goddess-like beauties, are so used to men hitting on them hard that the opposite strategy is sometimes the best way to go. "I could tell this guy liked me by the way he was smiling and asking me lots of questions at a party," says Moira, 23, a model in Los Angeles. "But he was keeping space between us at all times and kept the conversation on current events and TV; he wasn't prying to see if I had a boyfriend. He did ask if I wanted to go for a walk, but then he didn't put his arm around me or try to hold hands. By the time he finally kissed me at my car—and he even kissed me in slow motion—I was dying for him. I ended up asking *him* if he wanted to go out."

Keep her laughing. Ever notice how so many women are so earnest and uptight? Well, we all love men who can roll out the laughs and keep us giggling—a talent that can make up for a million physical shortcomings. "He is short and I'm tall, so I thought no way," says Renee, 28, a Web designer in Palo Alto, California. "But he forwarded me a hilarious E-mail, and then

GOING THROUGH THE AGONIZING "SO WHAT DO YOU DO?" AND "HAVE I SEEN YOU HERE BEFORE?" IS THE CONVERSATION-SPARKING EQUIVALENT OF SOGGY MATCHES.

when we were working late he told me these hilarious stories about our coworkers. Honestly, he's not that funny, but he kept relaying other people's humor, reminding me of funny *Seinfeld*s and taking me to crazy cabarets. I now own five pairs of flats, because I'm still dating him!"

Show her that you can look after her. If the bartender smiles when you come in, the busboys and underlings greet you, and she sees you help strange people locate the rest room, it makes her feel confident that you're a good guy who forms relationships with people. "I was at a mobbed concert with a girlfriend, and we couldn't figure out how to get up to the balcony," shares Gail, 25, an actuarial scientist in Des Moines. "This guy and his friend saw us looking bewildered and then told us that the balcony was so full we'd never be able to see. They knew a guy who worked at the auditorium who let us cut around back and sneak up to the front area near the stage." Without actually hitting on Gail, the guy stuck by her side all night, making sure she could see and getting her drinks. "When everyone had cleared out, he said, 'Do you want to see the balcony now?' He'd been such an upstanding gentleman all night that his risqué suggestion seemed totally acceptable."

Don't let a smile and an eye pass you by. Sometimes women can size you up and within a few seconds be pretty sure they're open to your advances. So if she holds your gaze in an elevator, on the way out of a party, or in a doughnut store, it never hurts to try to make the connection. The key is to keep it simple. "This sweet guy in shorts and a T-shirt was standing across the street from me waiting for

BARTENDER BABES SHARE THE LINES TO AVOID

We just couldn't trust scientists and psychologists and other overeducated ivory-tower brains to provide expert advice on a topic as important as The Pick-up Line. So we took a company-funded bar crawl—er, research mission—to ask sexy female bartenders the worst lines they'd ever heard. Honest to God, some guys said these things. We're so glad it won't be you...

Lines that tell her you're a one-track-mind horn dog:

"Are you wearing any underwear?"

"Can I take you home and suck on your toes?"

Lines that tell her she must look like a dumb slut:

"Hey, sweetheart, breakfast is on me."

"Can I charge that tab to my room? I don't have a room, but if you'll join me, I'll get one."

Lines that tell her you've been listening to too much Yanni:

"I know your father is a thief, because he stole the stars from the sky and put them in your eyes."

"You took my breath away. Can I have it back?"

Lines that tell her you think you're The Fonz:

"Does your boyfriend tell you how beautiful you are? 'Cause if he doesn't, I will."

"Let me have this to go. And you can wrap yourself up as well."

the walk light," says Madison, 29, a writer in San Francisco. "We made eye contact, smiled at each other as we passed, and then we both turned and caught each other looking back at the other. I burst out laughing at how obvious we were both being, and he ran back across the street and said, 'This is so weird, but if you're not seeing anyone, I'd love to give you my number. I'm not a criminal, and we could meet for coffee in a very public place.'" She went, and although she refused to tell her friends the real story of how they met, they carried on a fun-filled affair for the better part of a year.

Mesmerize Her
With Your Voice in 60 Seconds

Women are pretty obsessed with men's mouths. "As we're talking, I'm wondering, *What will his lips feel like when we kiss? What will his mouth feel like when he goes down on me?*" says Sadie, 32, a documentary film producer in Portland, Maine. So make the most of your mouth, specifically your voice, which experts say is a key romantic resource.

"Many people don't realize what a powerful tool your voice can be," says Joan Irvine, the clinical hypnotherapist. Here are her three steps to melting a girl's ears.

Step #1: Lower your voice slightly.
A deeper voice is reassuring and reminds a woman of how her dad used to take care of her. Also, women do tend to think the lower the voice, the manlier the man. Sorry, Mike Tyson.

Step #2: Use a subtle, singsong rhythm.
You don't want to sound like bad Japanese pop music, but without any inflection, she'll think that you're a one-note wonder in life—and, by extension, in bed. Try to emphasize one or two words in each sentence, and end your phrases on an upbeat note, not trailing off into mumble land.

Step #3: Slow your speaking pace.
It sounds simple, but if you're at all nervous, you run the risk of rambling on at a crazy Jim Carrey rate. Talking slower relaxes her and makes you seem more confident and patient. "A soothing voice will soon cause her to match her breathing rhythm to yours, and you'll have established an unconscious connection with her," swears Irvine.

How to Read Her Palm

When you want to impress the girl with your sensitivity but there's not a puppy in sight, nothing does the trick like palm reading. Keep in mind that it's too contrived just to waltz up to her and offer your services as Hand Man the Great, so try this subtle move: As she runs her hand through her hair or raises a palm to get the bartender's attention, stare at her hands until she says, "What are you looking at?" Then say, "Oh, a friend showed me how to read palms, so I've been noticing them lately." No member of the horoscope-obsessed gender will be able to resist sticking out her paw...and presto, you've got her.

Do you have to be a shaman to do it? No, as the pinnacle of Gypsy science, palm reading is easy—the three lines cutting horizontally across a woman's palm tell you all you need to know about her. Just grasp her hand firmly in one of yours and stroke it smoothly with your fingers as you work your wizardry.

The heart line is the one of the three closest to the fingers. If it starts near her index finger, tell her she's spiritual and difficult to please; if it starts under her middle finger, she's calm and mellow. A straight heart line indicates she's in control of her emotions; a curved one means she's sensual and hard to predict.

Just below the heart line you'll find the head line. If it's short and straight, the woman is ambitious and focused; if it's long and arching, extending almost to the pinkie side of her palm, it shows a supersensitive nature—she's subject to overpowering passions. (Jump her now.)

The life line, the one farthest from the fingers, starts halfway between her thumb and index finger and arcs downward to the wrist. The closer it stays to the mound of the thumb, the more of a homebody she is; if it veers away into the palm, it hints at an adventurous spirit (maybe she'll try that thing with the bungee cords you read about once). A break in the life line means that a dramatic event will drastically change her life. At what age? The line, long or short, represents her total life span, so if the break is, for example, a third of the way in from the life line's thumb-index "birth" end, she should expect a radical life-changing occurrence around age 30 or so. Can interruptions in this line be used to predict animalistic, life-changing sex in the extremely near future? Use your own discretion, bad boy.

RESEARCH SHOWS THAT WHEN YOU GET A GAL TALKING ABOUT SOMETHING HAPPY FROM HER PAST SHE'LL TRANSFER THOSE THRILLED FEELINGS ONTO YOU.

Icebreaker Gimmicks
That Won't Fail

The first step when approaching your babe of choice is to show her you're not a serial killer. But even after you've assured her that you don't keep vats of acid under your bed, you still have to shine brighter than all the other guys who aren't serial killers at the bar. Why are offbeat antics sometimes the best? "Women like a guy who can step out and do something creative," says Samuel Shem, coauthor of *We Have to Talk: Healing Dialogues Between Men and Women* (Basic Books, 1999). With this in mind, a handful of bold *Maxim*

HOW TO MAKE YOUR JOYLESS JOB SOUND GENIUS

Figured out that your mindless drone job isn't going to reel in the babes? Here's how to make even the most mind-numbingly dull occupation seem like you're making the whole world safe for democracy, Superman-style, every damn day.

Tip #1: Don't be half-hearted or dismissive about what you do.

Your own enthusiasm is her first—and sometimes only—clue as to how excited she should be about your job. An insurance claims adjuster impressed Julia, 32, an art gallery owner in Santa Fe, New Mexico, with this explanation: "Like firemen and detectives, I'm called in when someone dies or when a building mysteriously burns to the ground. Every day is a new adventure, a puzzle to solve." Julia explains, "He found a way to make insurance sound exciting—imagine what he could do with the missionary position!"

Tip #2: Emphasize the human side of your business.

She's looking for a people person who will impress her friends—and if you're a student of people, she'll want to start studying you a little closer. Liza, 26, an artist in Sarasota, Florida, who swore she'd never date a "suit," hooked up with a banker after he explained his job like this: "'It's not so much a numbers game as a people's game,' he told me. 'I love to go into businesses and learn how other people work.' After he said that, I knew he'd be willing to listen to my theories on cognitive neuroscience."

Tip #3: Dazzle her with your future climb to fame.

If you're making low dough or still have a job with the word *assistant* in it, you need to show her your ladder-climbing potential. "I met a guy who was a lowly researcher on a TV show," says Angela, 29, a manager at a travel agency in Rochester, New York. "But when I asked him what he wanted to do next, he said, 'It goes like this: researcher, associate producer, producer, executive producer, vice president of programming, network head honcho.' I thought, *Wow, I'm sticking with him—he's headed for the top!*"

---

editors road-tested a few moves that women said made guys stand out from the crowd (in a good way).

The gimmick: The pajama game

What you do: Wear some matching, clean pajamas and a nonratty bathrobe to a bar (and bring along some normally dressed buds). You'll get the same effect from most Halloween-type costumes.

Why it works: This unusual outfit shows a woman you have a sense of humor and serious guts.

Bonus tip: If she's too freaked out, tell her you just came from a charity event—she'll think you're a cool, crazy eccentric like Bruce Wayne.

The gimmick: Bar-stool poetry

What you do: Jot down a title of a poem ("Why I Love Beer Pretzels" or "Ode to Homer Simpson") and then have your buddy write a poem to fit your title, and so on.

Why it works: Women will wonder what you're writing and laughing about (laughing is key) and come over to see. Once they see you're literate, even oddly poetic, they'll

THE CHICK POP CULTURE CRASH COURSE

It's counterproductive to pretend that you like chick movies, chick books, etc., too much—any willingness to discuss soap operas tells her you're going to be her new best gay friend. "No man should gush about *Titanic* or *The English Patient*," declares John Sellers, author of *PCAT: Preparation for the Pop Culture Aptitude Test* (Little, Brown, 1998). "On the other hand, you may want to hold back on what you're really thinking—'Let *The English Patient* die already!' and 'Leonardo DiCaprio looks like something that someone ate and spat out'—in case they're her favorite flicks." To help you navigate her world, check out this Cliff's Notes of chick pop culture, compiled by Sellers and our unofficial poll of hot women coming out of the movie theater after seeing *As Good As It Gets.*

Chick Films

When Harry Met Sally...

Billy Crystal, who says that men and women can never be just friends, ends up marrying Meg Ryan after 10 years of palling around.

She digs it because: She identifies with Sally, who endures various circles of girl hell—she has lots of bad hair days, gets dumped, finds out her ex is getting married, and sleeps with her guy friend (Crystal), who then wigs out.

Bonus info: Carrie Fisher costars. All women dressed up as Princess Leia for Halloween as kids and love her.

Pretty in Pink

Not-so-rich Molly Ringwald falls for wealthy fop (Andrew McCarthy), while her offbeat guy friend, Duckie (Jon Cryer), tries, and fails, to woo her.

She digs it because: Ringwald is so independent and brave. She *sews her own perfect prom dress out of scraps* and bravely goes to the prom alone, where the rich boy gets a clue and takes her back.

Bonus info: In the original edit of the film she ends up with Duckie, but it was reshot so she got the rich guy in the end.

Chick TV

Ally McBeal

Boston lawyer Ally sometimes still pines for her coworker/ex-boyfriend who is married to her other coworker. Ling is a ruthless but sexy Asian lawyer who women admire but are scared of.

She digs it because: Ally is superthin and can wear micro skirts that real human women only wish they could. She has biological-clock issues and dances around with a computer-generated dream baby (which makes women relieved that they aren't completely insane).

Bonus info: The show features the first and only unisex bathroom in corporate-TV land.

Friends

Six friends hang out in a really clean New York City apartment, sometimes date one another and make surprisingly good sarcastic jokes.

She digs it because: The three women represent different parts of her. Monica is her anal side; Rachel is her high-maintenance princess side; and Phoebe is her New Agey, last-to-get-the-joke side. Note: She will never admit this is why she watches the show.

Bonus info: Rachel and Ross have shagged, as have Monica and Chandler. The original first-season script called for Monica and Joey to get together, but they never have.

Chick Music

Alanis Morissette

She sang the angry anthem "You Oughta Know," which includes lyrics asking her ex-boyfriend if his new girlfriend would, like her, "go down on you in a theater." Hello, bitter?

She digs it because: Alanis' songs pull on babe heartstrings and talk about things like "rain on your wedding day" (every woman's deepest fear).

Bonus info: She wore a skintight, nearly invisible unitard in her "Thank You" video, which chicks cheered on as part of the bony-Kate-Moss backlash.

Lilith Fair

An estrogen-enhanced Lollapalooza tour that featured crunchy musical divas including Sarah McLachlan, Sheryl Crow, Jewel, and other women who look like they could use a good bout of extended play.

She digs it because: The concerts are the grown-up girlie equivalent of slumber parties—you can laugh, you can cry, you can rage, you can do mud masks.

Bonus info: It's called Lilith Fair after the Bible's first woman, the strong-willed Lilith, who was exiled from Eden and replaced with the malleable Eve.

dump the guy they're playing pool with (a tawdry, 50-cent biker game that pales in creative comparison) to join you.

Bonus tip: Don't try to be Shakespeare—she'll think thee a sissy. Instead, include a funny line about your dog or your boss or your first bicycle that will yield a more personal conversation so you can put down the pen and pick *her* up.

The gimmick: Quiz show

What you do: Bring a deck of trivia cards and turn it into a "loser buys the next round" drinking game.

Why it works: It says you're interested in her brain, not just her body. Plus, you're able to buy her a drink without having it seem like a sleazy come-on.

Bonus tip: If you don't have a deck of trivia cards handy, build a card house from business cards—and ask her if she'll lend hers. Bingo! You've got her number.

How to Date the Temp

It's stated there quite plainly in the Ten Commandments of Work: Thou shalt not date thy office mate. (Think of the mess when one of you inevitably dumps the other.) Unless, of course, she's a temp. "The temp is one of the best dating scams going," claims Sparky (not his real nickname), a 29-year-old TV producer in New York City who hooked up with a two-week freelancer and continued dating her after she finished the job.

TALKING SLOWER RELAXES HER AND MAKES YOU SEEM MORE CONFIDENT AND PATIENT.

Temps tend to be young, eager, and used to shabby treatment (so you'll look like a prince). Best of all, she'll come and go with no messy strings attached...in theory, anyway. "My experience was moderately horrifying," admits Big Ed (not his name, either), a 28-year-old financial analyst whose drunken dalliance with a part-timer turned his workplace into a furnace of mortification after she spilled intimate details of their debauched evening to the typing pool. Here's advice on finessing the part-time lover from veteran temp-daters and Judy Kuriansky, Ph.D., author of *The Complete Idiot's Guide to Dating.*

Delay your pleasure. Unless the feeding frenzy for the new temp is overwhelming, don't pounce on your first sighting. "When Karen started, the first thing I found out was when she was leaving," remembers Sparky. Making your move on her last day plays the temp advantage to the hilt: You avoid interoffice mayhem, and if it doesn't work out, your problem has already disappeared.

Keep your distance. "Proximity does get the pleasure chemicals going," admits Dr. Judy, "but try to make sure you're not dealing with that person every day. A different area or even a different floor works better." Why? Because a clandestine office affair can easily be exposed by the tiniest public show of affection—which is hard to resist if you're two desks away. The bottom line: Hit on the new girl upstairs in accounts before making a move on your boss' interim secretary.

Stay away from interns. Haven't the men of this country learned this lesson yet? Extreme youth, beauty, inexperience, and a naive willingness to join you for drinks may be irresistible, but one misstep and you'll be branded a ruthless coyote. One worker—a 27-year-old lawyer from Baltimore who we'll call Bill—took an intern out to the opera; a few months later, he learned that the next round of interns had been warned by someone about the sleazy guy who was going to try to "Oval Office" them.

Beware of boomerangs. "After I hooked up with Karen, she came back about three weeks later," cautions Sparky. "We had to keep it under wraps for a month." But Sparky was fortunate: They were a congenial match. You may not be so lucky. Even worse for failed affairs, some temps become permanent fixtures. "My general advice," says Dr. Judy, "is to be really, really careful in the office." Those hard office desks can be rough on her back.

WHERE THE GIRLS REALLY ARE

Improving your chick yield starts with breaking out of the male-dominated singles bars and improving your odds. "You want to eliminate the competition," says Richard Gosse, chairman of the American Singles Association and author of *You Can Hurry Love* **(Marin Publishing, 1997). "So put yourself in places with the most women and the fewest men." Think about where your female friends hang out. If paint-your-own-pottery shops seem too girlie, bring along a sister or gal pal to legitimize your presence to other women. "Consider aerobics, or yoga, or arts and crafts," says Gosse, who knows one fella who actually enrolled in a college course called Understanding PMS. "This guy was the only man in a class of 50 women, and they were all complimenting him on being so sensitive to women's problems," says Gosse. Other ideas:**

Where: Weddings
Why: Weddings are great because women are feeling romantic (and a little jealous that their same-age friend, the bride, has already snagged her prince). Only here can you get away with asking a woman you've never met to dance before you've even said hello.

Where: The gym
Why: It's the best of both worlds. It's a sweaty, physical, grunting, spandex-filled fantasyland, yet it's as familiar as home, and if she sees you there regularly, she'll start to think you're A-OK. Try joining her volleyball or Tae-Bo classes: You'll have something in common and shut out the weight-room meatheads.

Where: A yoga class (They probably offer them at your gym, but you'll find more babes and less guys at dedicated yoga studios.)
Why: The women there will be sensual, calm, and flexible, and they'll at least be aware of the existence of superorgasmic Tantric sex.

Where: A shoe store
Why: While pretending you need some new dress shoes for work/a wedding/your parents'

How to Land a Babe at Work Without Getting Canned

Despite the fluorescent lights and the buttoned-up outfits, an estimated six to eight million people each year romp in the workplace. "Over half of what start out as office romances either become long-term or end in marriage," says Dennis M. Powers, author of *The Office Romance: Playing With Fire Without Getting Burned* (AMACOM, 1998) and a law professor at Southern Oregon University. "That's a much better percentage than the general population."

Picking her up will be quicker because you're a known quantity to her—after all, you're "the cute guy from work." Explains Pamela, 28, an accountant in Kansas City, Missouri: "I've dated two guys I've worked with, and it's very comfortable right away because you already have things in common and you can ask the girls who work with him if he's an OK guy." (The lesson: Be nice to female coworkers.)

True, many buzz-kill companies have fascist policies about interoffice dating, but the witch hunt seems to be breaking up. "Fears of sexual harassment suits are much greater than the reality," says Powers. "Even in boss-subordinate relationships, less than one out of 100 end in a legal dispute." If you must risk trouble with human resources, at least follow this wisdom from Powers and from real women who admit they've had sex at the office. (God bless 'em.)

anniversary party, you'll find stylish, financially solvent women who care about looking good. Feign (OK, admit) a moronic ignorance of everything having to do with shoes.

Where: A lingerie boutique
Why: Victoria's Secret is full of college students. For mature babes, try the department stores. To clear up the mystery of why you're there, just ask a prospective hottie which robe you should buy for grandma, who's in the hospital. ("Do you think a 70-year-old woman would prefer blue or yellow?")

Where: A tennis match
Why: A nonviolent sport with cute outfits? Sure, when smutty talk of "love" and "service" and "mixed doubles" fills the air. Tell 'em that you love football but find tennis a fascinating skill and strategy game...and then add in that it's so unfair for male tennis players to make more than female ones.

Where: A small party
Why: Unlike huge, anonymous parties, there will be a hostess to introduce (and endorse) you to all the single sweeties. You're automatically a "friend of a friend," not an anonymous rogue gate-crasher.

Where: The supermarket
Why: Women are thrilled by the idea of a man who shops and cooks. Crash your cart into hers (it gives you an excuse to apologize), or just ask her how to tell if this avocado is ripe (no woman who ever had a mother will be able to leave you there helpless in the produce aisle). Avoid telling her she has "a nice pear."

Where: A frou-frou beauty products store (e.g., Bath & Body Works, Aveda, or The Body Shop—which all have guy stuff like shaving cream, too).
Why: All the women there smell good and take care of their bodies. You should pretend you ran out of shampoo and just stumbled in.

Where: The Laundromat
Why: Given a choice between talking to you and watching her socks spin, it's likely she'll choose human interaction. Plus, women love watching men do their own domestic deeds. Again, feign helplessness (e.g., "Can I put these dark socks in here?"). It appeals to her nurturing nature, reassures her you're doing laundry for one, and even gives her a peek at your underwear.

Check out your company's rules on interoffice boinking. It's at the bottom of your file drawer, just under the fire-code regulations in that packet of stuff you got and ignored at your orientation. But you should also ask a few coworkers what the unofficial policy is. "It just made work so much more fun to go to a meeting and think to myself, *Wow, my manager did me from behind on this very boardroom table!*" says Marie, 23, an administrative assistant in Fresno, California. Is the ride worth the risk? Only you can decide.

Do a quick background check. Did she send around a psycho defamatory E-mail after her last breakup? Has she told the typing pool that she's dying to get pregnant? Did she photocopy her bare ass at the last Christmas party, and if so, where can you get a copy of it? "Gossip in any office is amazingly good stuff, so find out what you can about her," advises Powers.

Avoid the office sex bunny. Even if dating is "legal" at your firm, stay firm in your resolve not to date the secretary who has seen a lot of other corporate, um, members. She may look like an easy target, but realize that you'll be tainted in the eyes of the really great babes. "Four or five associate partners in our department have all dated this one Baywatch bimbo assistant," says Caroline, 25, who is currently dating her boss and is severely paranoid (and wouldn't E-mail us her home city). "The other lawyers and I all talk about how we would never date those guys—they're like male hoes." Whoa.

Anticipate leakage. Sex in the office is a messy business, and you can't keep an office romance secret in today's cubicle village. Why? Because there's a woman involved, and she'll eventually need to tell someone about the great sex she's having. If your office is informal and doesn't have rules against it, just confess and next week your liaison will be replaced by hotter gossip. If you're her superior and you suspect your relationship is about to be made public, do damage control. "The key rule is to tell the highest person you know who's above both of you first—bosses like to know what's going on," explains Powers. Then get cracking on updating your résumé!

chapter three

Seduce Her

Turn that date into something great.

Now that you've scored a hotter date than you deserve, what are you going to do with her? Answer: You're going to rock her world. Because whether she turns out to be your next big fling or just a three-night stand, blowing her away on those critical early dates will preserve your date-or-ditch option indefinitely. Get wishy-washy on her and she might just get bored and make the decision for you.

Fantastic dates keep her motor running because it's an early indicator of your potential for commitment. When a girl agrees to go on a date with you—unless it's a mercy date because she accidentally almost ran you over at the Quick-E-Mart—it's because she thinks, deep down, there's an outside chance you could be The One. "Most women usually have some kind of future in mind, and any man they date is auditioning for that future," explains Shari A. Betterman, Ph.D., a marriage and family therapist in Beverly Hills, California. "To women, having a boyfriend is a much closer step to marriage than having a girlfriend is to men."

That's a challenge: Unlocking a woman's doors means giving her plenty of evidence, from Date One right on up to the altar, that you just might be The One. Give her enough hope in those heady early days and you'll be free to climb her commitment ladder (she counts approximately 23 distinct steps between "guy I went out with once" and "boyfriend") at your own glacial pace, confident she won't dump you without two warnings and a fine.

All you have right now is a date...but at the end of this chapter you'll be a man with a plan. Here's what's going on in her head in those first hot-and-heavy courtship weeks and how you can turn it to your evil advantage.

Real Girls Spill Their Worst Dates Ever

A bad date is like a, well, bad date. You bite into it and immediately you want to hack it back out and spit it on the ground, but no-o-o, you have to be polite and chew it and swallow it and hope that nothing like it ever happens again.

To help you learn from your predecessors' mistakes, we girls rounded up the worst dates we've ever had and tried to distill just what went wrong.

> "A guy asked me out, but then he was late, so the movie I'd gotten excited to see was sold out. We decided to eat out instead, but we went to three restaurants and they all had one-hour waiting lists. Sure, if you've been dating someone for a while you can just laugh it off and go to McDonald's, but when I'm wearing a new skirt and lipstick, I don't want to play 'let's get to know each other over a Quarter Pounder with Cheese'—which is exactly what he suggested. Instead, we skipped dinner, had a drink, and didn't go out again." —Julianne, 32, lawyer, Minneapolis
>
> **the lesson:** Watching helplessly as the night falls apart around you shows you can't handle a simple crisis—and brands you a loser. Always have a backup plan: dinner reservations somewhere else, a nearby theater showing the same movie 15 minutes later, or a not-too-smoky bar, in case your angelic date is also asthmatic.
>
> "The worst was the guy who took me to a family wedding on our first date. I was hesitant to go, but he promised it'd be a quick, informal ceremony. It turned out to be a very long ceremony followed by a reception at this mansion with hundreds of people I'd never met. My date left to get us drinks while I tried to keep my smile plastered on and fumbled through all the questions about how long I'd known him ('Um, two days?'). I couldn't wait to get out of there, and never talked to him again." —Melissa, 25, copy editor, San Diego
>
> **the lesson:** Families, no matter how cool, should be kept out of the picture until the fourth or fifth date—there's too much pressure. Eventually, yes, she wants to go to a fun wedding with you, because it officially announces your couplehood. But not until you've gotten to know her so well that you'll want to hang with her and guide her past the rough spots (e.g., your lecherous Uncle Louie).
>
> "I agreed to go to the opera with a guy I'd met a few times who'd bought these expensive tickets right before his girlfriend broke up with him. When we met up, he started telling me all about his terrible day in the city, and how his car got towed,

and how it was costing him all this money. So I decided to be nice and order the least expensive item on the menu. Anyway, since he spent the entire meal telling me about his financial troubles, I offered to pay for the meal, almost jokingly. It was a totally empty gesture, but he said OK! I suppose I shouldn't have offered if I didn't mean it, but come on. I really was outraged that not only did I have to waste an evening with this pompous bore—who never even asked about my job—but that I also ended up paying for it, too!" —Sara, 26, writer, San Francisco

the lesson: If you asked her out, you must pay—end of story. Even if she asked you out, you must offer to pay and should strongly consider insisting on paying—unless she's really dying to pay, in which case let her. And always, always ask her at least two questions about her job and one about her family, or she'll think you're only interested in her breasts. (Don't ask her any questions about her breasts.)

"I brought this guy back to my apartment for a drink on our fourth date. We had only kissed once, so I had no intentions of sleeping with him, just making out a little on my couch. Anyway, we starting kissing and fooling around, and then suddenly his hands were inside my clothes, everywhere, so I stopped him and said I wasn't ready to move beyond that. He started telling me my logic was flawed and kept asking, 'Aren't you ever going to sleep with someone you didn't love first?' This guy knew almost nothing about me, so I don't know where that came from. So I said, 'Well there's no way it's going to happen tonight.' And he said, laughing, 'It could if I wanted it to.' I truly believe he was just joking, he was that kind of guy, but joking about taking advantage of me is never funny. Even now it gives me the shivers to think about it. He called to apologize, but I never called back." —Shirley, 22, advertising assistant, New York City

the lesson: Never push the sex itinerary on a maiden voyage. You have to convince her with your heart, not your hands, and you risk being blackballed from all womankind if you try to push yourself where you're not welcome yet. Remember, we all talk to each other...constantly. Plus, there's that whole jail-time thing.

IF YOU ASKED HER OUT, YOU MUST PAY— END OF STORY.

"I dated a guy who always wanted to have 'dates' at two in the morning. He was a musician who worked late, so it wasn't totally unreasonable, but the message was: 'I don't like you enough to make real plans with you.' He might as well have said, 'Do you just want to come over to my house early in the morning and screw?' The one time I went I just felt sleazy and ended up not sleeping with him." —Kylie, 29, graduate student, Iowa City, Iowa

the lesson: Make a solid effort to make her feel special and important. If she suspects even for a minute that you're inviting her over just to, um, service you, that's the last thing she'll want to do. A related tip: Women hate being "summoned"—you can score big points just by picking her up or heading to her crappy neighborhood for a date, because it shows you're willing to go out of your way for her.

First-Date Rookie Mistakes

In a singles' world full of borderline psychos and self-absorbed assholes, a guy can usually score at least a second date just by being unarmed and potty trained. But it is possible, even with our low expectations, for you to screw it up royally. We asked the gals to help us identify the rookie mistakes guys are prone to make early on in the dating game. The dating don'ts that make *Family Feud*-style buzzers go off in her head:

Showing up late. It's a double whammy of a screw-up. First, it tells her this date isn't important to you, and second, that you're scatterbrained and untrustworthy. If you're meeting her at the venue, you can add a third nasty side effect: You've left her flying solo and looking like a loser in front of the mocking gaze of completely disinterested strangers. (Don't ask.) Can't avoid being late? At least don't compound the mistake by trying to brush it off: She'll expect a reasonable excuse and for you to apologize profusely. Do it and you're off the hook.

IT ONLY TAKES A LITTLE PRO-ACTIVE PRINCE CHARMING ACTION TO GET HER KITH AND KIN MARCHING TO THE BEAT OF YOUR DRUM.

Showing up early. At her place, anyway: Any girl who has to answer the door with hot rollers in her hair will be pissed that you cut short her primp time. If you get to her door more than five minutes early, take a hike around the block—or, better, pop into a shop and pick up a little something for her. Flowers are nice.

Not making a reservation for dinner. Even if you get there and it's empty, you'll score points for being hyperprepared. If you didn't think about it and now there's a 60-minute wait, that's a whole hour for her to obsess over your lack of foresight.

Dressing too casually. Even if you're going to a baseball game, don't show up wearing torn jeans and a ratty T-shirt. She'll assume you dress that way all the time—and that a date with her ain't nothin' special.

Bragging and talking about yourself too much. Early on in the dating process, it's more like tennis than conversation: Ask her questions about herself, then nod and prod until she starts asking you questions back; continue until check arrives.

Blowing your nose in your napkin. That's monkey shit, man. Ask her if she has a Kleenex (chicks usually do), then excuse yourself and go to the restroom and blow your nose. Not only will you *not* offend her, but you'll also pick up points for excessive politeness.

Ordering a messy meal. This includes spaghetti, lobster, and those slippery steamed dumplings that slide off your chopsticks and splash soy sauce over a five-table radius. Your food foible will generate big laughs around her conference room tomorrow—and humiliating giggles all night. Instead, stick to a solid, dependable chunk of fish or meat you can keep on your fork.

Not having enough cash. Most women have been out with guys who discovered the hard way that Visa isn't everywhere they want to be. This sends any or all of the following date-killing messages: You're poor, you're disorganized, you're a dependent personality, this date was an afterthought for you, you may be a hobo. Asking to borrow money from your date, even if you pay her back right afterward, means the ATM will probably be the last place you see her.

Talking about past relationships. There's no way to mention an ex without making it look like you're not over her. If your date quizzes you about your last girlfriend, just state how long you dated in a matter-of-fact way, and emphasize that it's definitely over now. Surprise: That's all she really wants to know!

Be The Master of Your Domain

Remember that scene in *There's Something About Mary* in which Cameron Diaz is about to unhook her bra in front of that open bedroom window? Man, was that cinema or what? OK, but seriously: Remember that scene where Chris Elliott tells Ben Stiller he should whack the weasel before his big date with Mary so he won't come across like a big ol' horn dog?

Does this strategy stand up to expert scrutiny?

"It's a great idea," declares Joan Irvine, coauthor of *Recipes for Hot Sex*. "It gets that basic need taken care of." Women swear that if you're too excited to see them they can smell your sexual desperation. "It makes me think he hasn't had sex since Milli Vanilli and that my presence there is interchangeable with an inflatable doll," says Sandra, 27, a research assistant in Lincoln, Nebraska.

So go ahead, take a moment with Mr. Bojangles before you pick up your gal— just don't let on to her, your buddies, and especially us at *Maxim* that you did it.

One-Step Tips to Charm Everyone in Her World

As a guy, you'll be deciding all by yourself whether you want to see this girl again. Her decision, on the other hand, is likely to be made by committee: Her girlfriends, family, coworkers, and even the gay pizza delivery boy will all have meaningful input into whether or not you get a second shot with her. (We didn't say it was fair.)

The odds may seem hopelessly stacked against you, but there's an opportunity here. It only takes a little proactive Prince Charming action to get her kith and kin marching to the beat of *your* drum. Here's how to woo the "extras" in her life, who will serve as a droning chorus constantly reminding her what a great catch you are.

Her mom | the angle: She wants to know you'll keep her daughter clad in the finery she's become accustomed to. Emphasize how hard you're working to climb the ladder. "Hi, Mrs. P! Wish I could stay longer, but when it comes to extra commissions, I'm all about work."

Her dad | the angle: All he cares about is making sure you're not being a jerk to his little girl, particularly cheating on her like that last little bastard, what's-his-name. Respectful adoration is the key. "Debbie's about as close to perfect as a human can get. Believe me, I'm well aware how lucky I am to be with her."

Her best friend | the angle: She wants to know you're the kind of guy who'll generate great romantic tales that'll be shared on girls' nights out. So ladle it on thick: "When I first saw Debbie it was like alarm bells went off in my head. I had to ask her to repeat her name because I was so blown away by her...presence."

Her brother | the angle: He just wants to know that, as a potential future family member, you're cool and will be an ally in interfamily flare-ups. Just feign interest in whatever he does—golf, tennis, monster-truck shows. The correct answer is always, "Yeah, I'm into that, too."

Her coworkers | the angle: They just want the gossip, and don't care if it's good or bad, but their knowledge of her is so shallow and limited they'll be easily bamboozled by any observed romantic gesture. Make an effort to drop by her office, letting her know in advance so she can rally the troops, and make sure to bring a small bouquet of flowers or some small token. Even a tiny brownie will send the message she wants them to overhear, namely: "I'm always thinking of you."

Her cat | the angle: Cats are the basket cases of the animal kingdom—but remember, you're much bigger and smarter. According to the book *Psycho Kitty?* (Crossing Press, 1998) by Pam Johnson Bennett, any kitty toy on a dangling string will make you shine like Dr. Doolittle. Why? Because, according to the book, "the cat redirects its aggression toward the toy at the end of the string, instead of at you."

LET YOUR ANSWERING MACHINE

We know what you're thinking: "Phone messages, for Chrissakes? I gotta worry about that, too?" The answer's yes: As Wellesley College associate psychology professor Linda Carli, Ph.D., told millions of *Glamour* readers in a recent article: "His answering-machine greeting can give you a big clue to his personality because it's very often an extension of himself." The article went on to tell women how to deconstruct and decode men's messages. We're here to help you use that information for evil.

Your outgoing message: Music blasting, roommates yelling, and the crowd at Wrigley Field cheering through your TV speakers.

What it says to her: You still think the frat is where it's at, and your bathroom probably doesn't have toilet paper.

More chick friendly: If you like having a personalized message with some background noise, then put on something softer but cool that you don't have to yell over, like Lenny Kravitz or Elvis Costello.

Your outgoing message: Short and not-so-sweet, such as, "Not here, message me!" or just, "You know the drill—do it after the long beep."

What it says to her: You don't have time for social pleasantries. (And some super-analyzers may find it code for "premature ejaculator"—yikes!)

Her dog | the angle: The trick to keeping Spot's teeth out of your ass is to avoid making eye contact until after you've let him smell the back of your hand, advises Jim Keenan, owner of Keen Dog Training. Soon you'll be rolling him over on his back and rubbing his tummy—and she'll be swooning, since all pet owners believe their pets are uncanny judges of character.

Her kids, or nieces and nephews | the angle: The little dickens are always craving attention, so give it to them. "Eye contact will let children know you're focusing your interest on them and not treating them casually," says Anita Gurian, Ph.D., senior psychologist at the New York University Child Study Center. Bribery, in the form of candy, action figures, PlayStation games, and cold, hard cash, rarely hurts your cause.

ALWAYS HAVE A BACKUP PLAN: DINNER RESERVATIONS SOMEWHERE ELSE, A NEARBY THEATER SHOWING THE SAME MOVIE 15 MINUTES LATER, OR A NOT-TOO-SMOKY BAR.

Send Her the Right Message With the Message You Leave

1. Sound upbeat. There's no need to overgush and scare her, but sound like you're glad to be calling, not like it's a chore. Remembering to smile as you talk helps.

2. Don't talk for too long. Remember Jon Favreau in *Swingers* and his desperate phone disaster? Don't emulate that. The instant you realize you're rambling, acknowledge it so she'll accept that you're not insane, and then cut yourself off. Just say, "OK, I'm just rambling here—give me a call, 555-5555. Talk to you later."

3. Dangle a carrot. Mention at least one specific thing from your most recent conversation together—it makes her think she's been on your mind ever since. It can be as simple as, "Hey, I figured out who starred in that Hitchcock movie—call me back."

DO THE TALKING FOR YOU

More chick friendly: Go with the standard: "Hi, it's Joe Blow. I'm not in right now, so leave me a message at the tone." Explains Julia, 33, a hairstylist in New York City, "If the message is too quick, you can't tell if it's him. I didn't leave a message the last time that happened!"

Your outgoing message: Overstating it. "Hi, you've reached Joe Blow. Please leave your name, number, the time of your call, and a brief message after the tone. When you're finished, press the star key, or if you'd like to re-record, press the pound key."

What it says to her: That you're either a control freak or that she's reached Les Nessman at WKRP. Either way, it says to her that you'll be as exciting in bed as Mr. Rogers.

More chick friendly: If it feels natural to you to have a longer message, then cut down on the weirdness and add some courtesy. "I'm not in, but I'll return your call at my earliest convenience. Thanks!"

4. Keep it casual... Say something like, "Give me a call back, even if you just want to chat or whatever." Explains Petra, 24, a restaurant manager in Dallas: "I worry that if I call back, a guy will automatically assume I want another date. Last spring I was taking a hiatus from dating, but I called back this cute guy I'd met at work anyway, since he said he just wanted to gab—he was so much fun that my hiatus ended pretty quickly!"

5. ...but be specific. If you want her to call you back, say so—act too casual and she won't know what the next move is. "I want to be told specifically," says Susan, 26, a photo researcher in Boston. "If he just says, 'Hey, just checking to see how you're doing,' I wonder, *Well, is it my move now, or is he going to call again?*"

Caller ID: How Long Before You Can Reach Out and Touch Someone?

Her shawl of scrutiny extends beyond just what you say—she also analyzes how long you wait to call her and labels you as a result. Here's a sneak peek at her time line. If you call...

One hour after you've met: This tells her that you're obsessing over her already, and she should probably put the chain on the front door. Unless she left her insulin in your car, there's no excuse for a call this quick.

One day after you've met: She'll think you're keen but not crazy, as long as you have a reason for ringing so soon—say, a concert you want to take her to that you need to reserve tickets for. Call again the following day, though, and you risk reverting to the stalkerish one-hour status (see above).

> **"DEBBIE'S ABOUT AS CLOSE TO PERFECT AS A HUMAN CAN GET. BELIEVE ME I'M WELL AWARE HOW LUCKY I AM TO BE WITH HER."**

Two to three days after you've met: She'll be starting to get a little concerned, but will have made 8,000 excuses for you to explain her silent phone. It's perfect: Now you've built suspense, and she'll be in a lather when you get her on the line.

One week after you've met: You'd better have been captured by pirates: This is a long time to keep a lady waiting, and she'll want a good explanation as to why you never picked up any of the 1,000 conveniently located telephones you've presumably passed in the last seven days. The only excuse is a flatter-filled one that tosses the ball back in her court: "I've been wanting to call and ask you out, but I just wasn't sure if you were into it."

How to Get the Competition to Take a Dive

Isn't it romantic: You, the girl of your dreams...and some loser she can't or won't shake off? You won't be able to sleep at night—not in her bed, anyway—until you can first get her to ditch any other guys she's currently dating. "It seems like I often end up with a couple of guys hanging around," says Gillian, 30, a graphic designer in Ames, Iowa. "I usually let it go on this way for a while and see how they handle it —and how they handle it usually makes my decision of who stays and who goes." So here, straight from the mouths of babes, are great tips on convincing her to cut that other no-good jerk-off loose.

Step #1: Show her your stuff.

In your one-on-one talks with her, find excuses to talk about your strengths and Dickhead's shortcomings. Use backhanded, subtle comments like: "I really envy Joe's ability to make ends meet on his salary. Personally, I don't think I could do it."

FIRST-DATE FOLLOW-UP MOVES
THAT GUARANTEE DATE #2

So you've made it through that all-important first date? Don't kick back yet, Casanova: These postgame moves will significantly boost your odds of earning a sequel.

Flowers are good...but flowers at work with which she can lord her good fortune over all her coworkers are better.

Sounding surprised but pleased if she calls you first after the date is good...but sounding surprised and insanely thrilled is better.

Apologizing for the way her jacket got dirty when she rubbed up against your car is good...but writing an apologetic haiku on a napkin and reading it to her over the phone is better.

Sending her a "thanks for a fun time" E-mail is good...but sending her an electronic card from hallmark.com (as long as it isn't too mushy) is better.

A sweet phone call is good...but leaving a sweet message on her work voice mail after you get home from your date that she'll hear at her desk first thing in the morning is better.

Asking her where she wants to go on your second date is good...but sneakily finding out her favorite haunts and taking her there as a surprise is better.

Not making a huge deal out of the fact that she slept with you on the first date is good...but acknowledging that she gave you special access ("I must be the luckiest guy in the world") is better.

Mentioning to a mutual friend that you had a good time is good...but making a special point to call a mutual friend and berate him or her for not introducing you sooner (this guarantees she'll hear about it) is better.

But beware: Say anything too harsh and she'll get defensive on his behalf and take his side.

Step #2: Start sabotaging your rival.

If you've planted the seeds of doubt, tension will start to grow between Dipshit and your gal. He will be looking for answers—and you, his gal's new chum, will be in a prime position to besiege him with crummy advice. Tell him she hates public displays of affection; claim the surprise trip he's planning will only scare her off...you get the idea. If you don't know him personally, send these messages through a mutual friend in the network who's on your side. As you comb the romance out of their relationship, keep asking her, "What's wrong? You seem down lately..."

Step #3: Get her posse on your side.

The decision about which one of you is truly right for her is not her decision alone—not by a long shot. Her female friends have gathered around her like presidential advisers in the Oval Office during Desert Storm. A couple of lines that tell her girlfriends that you're the best of the bunch: "Have you talked to Debbie today? She seemed a little down last night, and I was worried," and "It sounds clichéd, but I knew the moment we met that she was unlike any girl I'd been out with before."

CATS ARE THE BASKET CASE OF THE ANIMAL KINGDOM—BUT REMEMBER, YOU'RE MUCH BIGGER AND SMARTER.

Step #4: Be there for her.

As your advice to him sours things and her gal pals pressure her to dump him, at some point the Dork King is going to get wise and stop listening to you. Suddenly your relationship with her—the deep conversations, the long walks, yadda yadda yadda—will start bugging him more than inflamed hemorrhoids on a six-month cattle drive. He'll tell her to stop seeing you; she'll accuse him of being an overprotective meathead; and she'll gravitate to you, the only guy who understands her.

Step #5: Be Alan Alda.

To seal the deal, become the most sensitive son of a bitch she's ever laid eyes on, especially as their budding young relationship goes supernova. If it seems like they're starting to get along again, stir things up by asking, "Whatever happened with that big fight you two had? I hope he apologized." The more she obsesses about what's wrong with her current guy, the sooner she'll realize she needs to spend more time with a guy like—hey, what are *you* doing Friday night?

Step #6: Finish him off.

Now that you've X'ed out her ex, make sure the palooka stays that way. The last thing you need is a guy who knows her really well reemerging every time you two have a spat. Choose a night when she's prying into your past or rambling on about her own, and then ask her why she and her ex split up so you can find out what she hated about him. Then, be the angel to his devil. If he used to interrupt her all the time, let her babble on. If he was a control freak, ask her what *she* wants to do all the time. By magnifying his faults, you'll make sure the fracture between them can never be healed.

Her Three-Part Test

Part 1: The party test

Your behavior at your first party as a couple is a critical barometer of whether you're worthy of the constant sex she'll be giving whomever she calls "boyfriend." It's an obstacle course of etiquette and loyalty issues, but you can easily ace this test with some training tips from real gals.

If it's your party, tell her at least a week ahead of time, more if she's a busy gal. "When a guy gives me advance notice, it shows that he realizes I have a life outside him—and that he really wants me there," says Michele, 22, a design student in Providence.

Give her a mini bio of the important people in your life who will be there. This specifically includes your best friend and any exes. She'll want to make a good impression, so be the man and blaze her a trail. "I realized halfway through the party that this woman I was talking to was his ex—and there I was quizzing her about him like an idiot!" says Rachel, 29, a writer in New York City. "I felt like he wasn't taking care of me, like I'd just been thrown to the lions. We broke up a few weeks later."

Visit and stray. She doesn't want you clinging to her apron strings, but she'll feel more loved if you establish that you two are at this party as a team. Be her drink man—keep coming back to make sure she's keeping her whistle wet—and pop in on her conversation once every 20 minutes to say, "Hey, have you seen the roof views?" or "Are you OK—do you want to stay another half-hour?" Make her feel like the belle of the bash.

If you're throwing the party, let her play hostess. It's not a burden; women actually love this. "I was hoping he'd ask me to decorate or help out. He didn't, so instead of feeling like the girlfriend, I just felt like any other guest," says Julia, 33, a hairstylist in New York City.

Give her a wink across the crowded room. Make eye contact from afar, or wave at her from the stairs. "I love it when I'm in a crowded room and I look up to see my boyfriend looking back at me," says Susan, 26, the photo researcher from Boston. "It means that even with all these party distractions, he's still thinking about me. Plus, it's a huge turn-on because it starts me thinking about taking him home!"

Part 2: Embracing her quirks

Early on in a relationship, her biggest fear is that you'll discover her eccentricities— her sardine-and-peanut-butter-sandwich habit, her webbed toes, her psychotic obsession with the Kurt Cobain murder conspiracy—and run away screaming. All the other guys, at best, have ignored her quirks or pretended not to notice. But the man who can *embrace* her weird ways is the man who'll truly win her heart—and all those fun parts, too. So here's how to play it.

SHE DOESN'T WANT YOU CLINGING TO HER APRON STRINGS, BUT SHE'LL FEEL MORE LOVED IF YOU ESTABLISH THAT YOU ARE AT THIS PARTY AS A TEAM.

Her weirdness: She has a bizarre mole, birthmark, scary leg veins.
Other guys have said: "Whoa—looky here!"
Instead, try: "Your mole? It looks like a little smiley face to me. Have you noticed that?" Explains Sarah, 29, a bartender in Kansas City, Missouri: "I have these spider veins on my thighs, and I was mortified a few years ago to see my new boyfriend staring at them at the beach. But then he just reached out and traced one with his finger from my thigh to my knee—and somehow turned my big horror into foreplay. Genius!"

Her weirdness: Collecting hundreds of troll dolls, ceramic body parts, souvenir spoons.
Other guys have said: "You know, you could actually use this room if you didn't need it to store all this crap."
Instead, try: "Have you tried eBay? I hear you can pick up valuable old trolls for pennies on the dollar!" Validate her obsession. If you can't get her to stop, you can at least monitor her addiction.

Her weirdness: She's obsessed with a celebrity or rock star.
Other guys have said: "You know, of course, that Ricky Martin has no idea you exist."
Instead, try: "How about I tape the Ricky Martin concert for you, and you come over and I'll make my special Ricky Martinis?" Don't worry, she won't expect you to adopt her obsession—but she'll love you for respecting it as a legitimate part of her.

Her weirdness: She's high maintenance when it comes to food, ordering seemingly random effluvia "on the side" and quizzing the poor waitress about how the sauces are prepared.
Other guys have said: "Can't you just eat already?" (Special alert: It could be that she's recovered from an adolescent eating disorder and has created funky food guidelines for herself to stay well. Find out by bringing up the topic of anorexia in a neutral context; she'll probably admit it if she's been there. If so, food is off-limits as chat unless she brings it up.) For non-eating-disordered gals...
Instead, try: "Watching you order a meal is like witnessing Middle East peace negotiations—maybe you should be an ambassador to something!" You've acknowledged her weirdness and poked a little normal fun, and now she's breathing a sigh of relief (as she counts calories in her head).

Her weirdness: An otherworldly sex-toy collection.
Other guys have said: "Are you some kind of sex addict? Not that that's a bad thing...anyway, I'm not sure this will hold us both."

Instead, try: "Hey, whatever warms your gravy works for me—do I wrap this around you or what?—but tomorrow night, *I'm* the bed master. Are you cool with that?"

Part 3: The hero test

Now, your third and final test: Will you be a reliable hero when she needs you? Sure, you're pretty certain you'd come up with the *cojones* if someone attacked her or if you had to get away from the mob or something. But little did you know that while you're waiting for that you-versus-the-mugger moment, real crises are popping up all around you. Instead of being annoyed or amused at her over-reactions to life's twists and turns, you can use these opportunities to prove what a sensitive Superman you are.

"It's difficult for men to be support-ive during a crisis because men are more likely to be solvers of problems than they are soothers of emotions," says Mark Goulston, M.D., a couples counselor for iVillage.com who also trains FBI agents to deal with hostage situations and suicide interventions. "But when she's feeling upset, she doesn't want a solution—she wants not to be upset anymore." So your job is not to solve the problem. All you need to do for hero status is prove to her that her feelings and her problems (even if it's just a bad hair day or a cellulite scare) are important to you. Here's how.

She's mad because her female nemesis stole an assignment she wanted. She's screaming, stamping her feet, throwing mascara wands.

Hero move: Stand next to her, nodding silently as she talks. (Don't raise your voice to tell her she's being irrational—she'll refocus her anger on *you*.) Then wait for her to crumple in your arms and cling to you.

Why it works: She'll wear herself out screaming, and the sight of you being Sean Connery calm will make her realize she's overreacting. All women want a man who's a rock in a crisis.

She's crying because her cat died, or she had a fight with a girlfriend or her mom, and now she's blubbering and talking in nonsensical half sentences.

Hero move: Rush to her and hold her. Make comforting noises, and say, "It's OK. You're OK now," to emphasize that the reason she's OK is because sensitive, strong Harrison Ford guy is here, baby.

Why it works: Even if she pushes you away, you still win. She wants to know that you aren't afraid of her tears—because guys in her past probably *were,* and that's the kiss of death.

She's pissy because she can't make a decision about what she wants to do, and when you ask what's wrong, her eyes roll back in her throbbing head and she shrieks, "Nothing, OK!"

Hero move: Keep it simple—anything you say will be held against you. Try: "Whatever's wrong, I'm here." Or, since by now hopefully you've learned what her favorite things are, suggest a specific comfort food, if only to remind her that you really do know her pretty damn well. If her pissiness continues, ask her if she wants you to go. She'll crack.

Why it works: The thought of you leaving makes her cling to you—when she's pissy she needs lovin' from someone she feels understands her. A selfless back rub is often a cure-all—and from there, it's a pleasantly slippery slope to her bed! (Just don't rush it, or you're dead meat.)

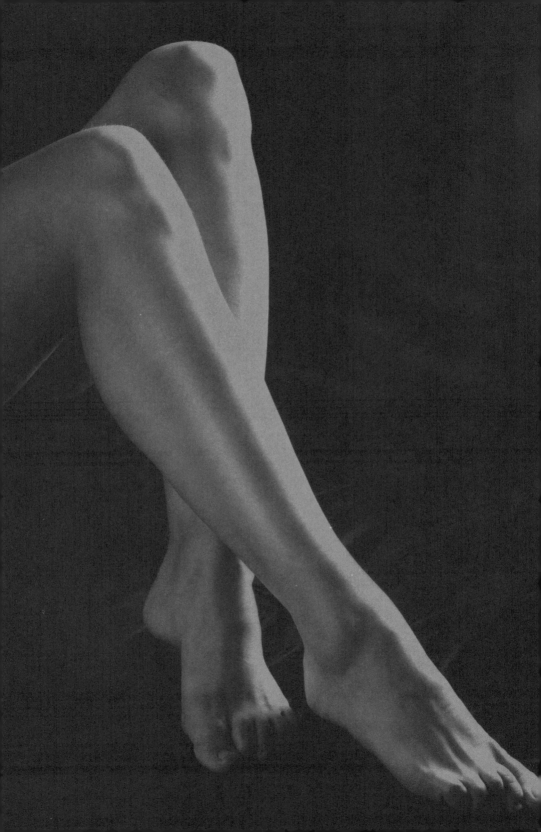

chapter four

Get Her Naked

Now that your new gal's putting on her best clothes for you, here's how to go about getting 'em off.

Figuring out how many innings you have to play before attempting to round her bases is always tricky. But you may not have to wait as long as you think to head for home: Women expect you to give it the old college try after three to six dates, explains Tracey Cox, author of the book Hot Sex: How to Do It *(Bantam Books, 1999). "By that time she's thinking,* Hey, why hasn't he made a move yet? Isn't he attracted to me? *And asking her if it's too soon reassures her that you think she's special enough to wait for," Cox says. "Play it right and the answer should be, 'No, let's do it right here!'"*

Still, her decision to get naked with you for the first time hinges on many things, from your apartment's decor to how good dinner was to her irrational fear that you'll think her butt is too big. Even if your dates have been a logical progression to this big night in the bedroom, things still have to be perfect before she'll drop cotton. "I usually know after the first or second time I meet a guy whether he's a man I'd want to sleep with," says Karen, 32, a photographer in Santa Fe, New Mexico. "But even though I've made that decision, the first night has to be right—I have to feel like he really likes me, I have to know I can trust him, and it doesn't hurt if there are candles and soft background music."

It's a mine field that calls for serious maneuvering—and just to keep things interesting, Mother Nature has rigged the game so that when your testosterone level hits DEFCON 4, your brain downshifts to automatic pilot. But the shortcuts and strategies that follow will give you your best possible shot at convincing your honey the time is right and the guy is you.

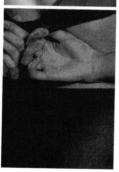

The Three Conversations
That Unlock Her Bedroom Door

Women experience peer pressure when it comes to sex, too. After a woman goes out with a guy a couple of times, her girlfriends will ask if he's "boyfriend material." That's chick-speak for, Do you feel you know him well enough to shag him silly yet?

When your sure thing surprises you by saying no, nine times out of ten it's because she's afraid she doesn't know enough about your past to defend her borderline sluttiness to her friends later. And why doesn't she? Because you foolishly keep running from the three conversations that will make gettin' jiggy with you A-OK.

Conversation #1: Your dating history. She doesn't want to know details like all of their names or whether they were multi-orgasmic. But she also doesn't want total, you-must-be-hiding-something vagueness. "I find myself holding my breath until I learn a guy's true back story to see if he's someone I want to share a bed with regularly," says Elise, 28, a makeup artist in Los Angeles.

At a minimum, your gal will want to be reassured that you've had at least one serious, multimonth relationship and that you're still friends with at least one ex-girlfriend. The combination shows that you can commit, forgive, and forget. She also wants to make sure there aren't any exes you're still pining for. But feel free to toss in a well-placed, "The breakup was hard. I was bummed for a while, but I've moved on." It shows you have emotional depth.

Conversation #2: Your childhood. She wants to know that you weren't fondled by priests, never killed small animals for thrills, and didn't get expelled from elementary school. She wants to know you had a happy childhood (i.e., you aren't predisposed to stalkerdom should the relationship go sour). That being said, it doesn't hurt to mention *one* traumatic childhood event (Did your parents get divorced? Were you the school outcast?) so she knows her nurturing skills won't atrophy, and so she can relate to you if her girlhood wasn't so happy. Finally, she wants to know that you liked/still like your folks—it shows you'll make a good dad someday. Yes, she's already thinking about things like that, even if only in the abstract.

Conversation #3: Your sexual beginnings. At what age did you first do it and with whom? Was it love? Was it good? Why the third degree? Be careful—this probe isn't about sex, it's about emotions and sensitivity. It's not important who, where, or what you shagged in your misspent youth; what matters is how you felt about it, how you handled problems, how you treated all the girls you've loved before.

So now that you know what she's looking for, tailor your answers accordingly. If you didn't lose you virginity until college, don't say, "To be honest, I couldn't find a willing partner." Instead, pick up sensitivity points with, "I just wasn't ready," or "I just hadn't found the right girl." If you lost it at 12, she'll be a little shocked, so mitigate the awful truth with an adorably vulnerable image: "I had no idea what I was doing." If you've forgotten the name of your first, make one up to reassure her that sex is a special thing that you don't easily forget.

Finally, before the first time you sleep together, she may ask if you've been tested. (You *have* been wearing condoms every time, right?) If she wants the two of you to get tested, the correct answer is, "Well, I'm sure I'm OK, but if it'll make you feel more at ease, I'm all for it." Don't hem and haw, make jokes, or get defensive about whether she thinks you're a huge guy slut: She's just heard those stories about prostitutes at bachelor parties and is understandably wary. Plus, guys lie all the time. Admit it.

America's Funniest Sexual Blunders

Women's biggest problem with first-time sex is nervousness. When accidents happen in the bedroom, it can send the mood out the window...or, with just a little James Bond resourcefulness on your part, it can set the stage for an anecdote she'll never stop telling even when she's 70. Our gals recall hilarious bedroom blunders—and the amazing ways guys turned disasters into all-star performances.

"As he was unbuttoning my blouse in his bedroom, I asked if he had condoms. He said yes, and then he cast a worried look around the room. He waited until we were buck naked to really start searching for the rubbers. Clothes were flying, drawers were being pulled out of the dresser. He ran back and forth to the bathroom twice, started pulling boxes out from under the bed—I was hugging a pillow and crying with laughter. He finally stopped, looked at the ceiling and said, 'God, why hast thou forsaken me?' I was shrieking. Raincoat-less, we ended up just giving each other, uh, oral pleasure that night. We had real sex for the first time the next night, after he'd hit the drugstore. And I think because of the hilarious antics of the previous night, my usual first-time jitters were nowhere to be found." —Paige, 24, nursing student, Houston, Texas

"We'd talked about how we wanted this night to be *the* night for sex, and he was breathing fast and hard from the

YOUR DECOR DECONSTRUCTED

The presence of a hot prospect in your pad means every smallest detail in your apartment is being analyzed for clues to your personality. Bottom line: Don't bring her over until you take a look at the messages she reads in the most innocent stuff...and redecorate accordingly.

- Picture of parents on dresser = Is sensitive and stable
- Collection of beer cans = Is still stuck in high school
- CDs are alphabetized = Can plan a successful family vacation
- Owns complete, masculine set of dishes and flatware = Knows how to cook
- TV is bigger than oven = Could be compensating for other crucial shortcomings
- Foosball table = Is boyishly charming, like Chandler and Joey
- Dining-room chairs that match = Invests in the future
- Rowing machine dominates living room = Has screwed-up priorities
- Shag carpet = Didn't realize *Austin Powers* was just a movie
- Pet = Is dependable; has ability to care for others
- Speakers mounted on walls = Is stable; has steady job
- Cardboard cutout of sports figure = Has "issues"
- Candles in actual candle holders = Is detail oriented; may have trust fund
- Monet print = May be a latent homosexual
- Dental floss = Comes from a good home
- Any room painted red = Is a sick fuck
- Fraternity paraphernalia = Will try to engage her in an act of depravity to win a bet with a friend
- No furniture = Is out drinking most of the time
- Lots of unmarked videos = Is an amateur pornographer
- Display of *Star Trek* model ships = Is unlikely to hold up his end of the relationship
- Mattress on floor = Doesn't get much action; may be chronic masturbater
- Rotting trash = Seeks mother figure desperately
- Copy of *Maxim* on coffee table = Is brilliant, funny, and tuned in

moment we entered my place. Unfortunately, I was nervous and I took a little longer to get going, so I was trying to slow things down a little. Finally, I could tell that he was in pain trying to hold back, so I whipped off my shirt and panties, moved down the bed to unzip his shorts, and as I did—*pow*—I got hit in the eye with his, well, his *excitement*. It really stung, and he was immediately apologetic. He got me Kleenex and water and helped me wipe it out of my hair. We talked and laughed about it, and then he went down on me for a very, very long time to make up for the disaster. We're still together and our routine usually involves him coming quickly (but not in my eye!); then it's my turn, then his turn again. Not bad, huh?" —Brianna, 24, events planner, Skokie, Illinois

"My life is stressful, so I need mellow music to help me relax and get in the mood. Anyway, at my boyfriend's apartment, he hit the dimmer on the lights and poured some wine, and I thought, *Right, tonight's the night.* So I got up to switch the music to something other than Dinosaur Jr., but he had no make-out music! I asked him to choose his mellowest CDs, but it was all too rock-raging for me. We continued to make out, and as we were taking each other's clothes off, I said, 'Look, let's just not have music.' But then I got freaked out because it was too quiet. So he looked up at me, sighed, and started singing, 'Kum-ba-yah, my Lord, kum-ba-yah...' as he kissed my stomach. I laughed and laughed, and then it dawned on us to try the radio. I'll never forget my orgasm, because just then the D.J. was saying, 'Woo-hoo, folks: Today we're going to have record highs!'" —Dawn, 21, student, Indianapolis

"I was relieved my first time with my boyfriend because he asked me how he should touch me. I was happy to talk him through it, but unfortunately, we didn't communicate well. I started out coaxing him 'left' and 'right' but he kept getting it wrong, so I started saying 'counterclockwise,' and I swear he lifted his head and looked at my clock. Finally, using 'east' and 'west' was working and getting me extremely excited. But when I get really close, I start fixating on whatever word is in my head, so there I was screaming, 'Oh, north, north!' and he's frantically trying to get it right, and he yells, 'Minnesota or Canada?' Somewhere near the border we hit the jackpot. We laughed about it at breakfast the next morning. Then he sent me a card at work the next day that said: 'North, south, east, west/It's Julie that I love the best. P.S. I'm available to lead guided tours to Canada at your pleasure.' What a guy." —Julie, 24, counselor, Columbus, Missouri

SHE WANTS TO KNOW THAT YOU WERE NOT FONDLED BY PRIESTS, NEVER KILLED SMALL ANIMALS FOR THRILLS, AND DID NOT GET EXPELLED FROM ELEMENTARY SCHOOL.

10 THINGS TO STOCK

1. Two clean towels. One for after sex, and another for her shower.

2. A full roll of toilet paper. Splurge on the soft, cushy kind.

3. A virgin bottle of water in the fridge so she doesn't have to worry about the cleanliness of your glasses.

4. A contact case and saline solution. If you're 20/20, pretend your brother left it so she doesn't get suspicious.

5. Condoms. And plenty of them.

Eight Stealth Moves
That Disarm Her Defenses

"Women are not going to feel comfortable if they sense the whole time that all you want to do is get them into bed," says Joan Irvine, coauthor of *Recipes for Hot Sex*. The key: Make us think you're not after sex at all. Our girls spill the romantic moves that secretly put them in the mood.

1. Undress her slowly. "I love it when a guy asks if it's all right to kiss you, or if he stops as he's unbuttoning your shirt and says, 'Is this OK?' It's like he's acknowledging that I'm the one in control and it's my choice," explains Dawn, 21, the Indianapolis student. "Of course, then I usually say, 'Sure, it's OK.'"

2. Compliment the underwear. If there's a chance she's going to have sex with you for the first time, a woman will choose her underwear combo carefully. "If I've agonized over whether he'll be more turned on by the black bra or the pink lace bra, it's a relief when he says, 'Wow, you look so beautiful in this.' Then he gets big points," points out Janelle, 28, a sales representative in Omaha.

3. Define the night as special. It'll sound contrived if you just blurt out, "This night is so special" à la Stuart Smalley. But she wants to know she's a prize you've been waiting for desperately, so do something to symbolically mark the moment as transcendent so she can justify "getting carried away" (i.e., letting you tear her clothes off). Get up and dim the lights, grab a handful of candles, or suddenly switch the wine for that champagne you forgot you had, explaining to her, "Hang on just a sec, I really want this night to be special."

4. Give her an entire day. This serves two functions. First, it shows her she's worth clearing your schedule for, from noon till dawn. Second, it gives her time to get dangerously relaxed around you. After you've playfully wrestled around on the grass in the park, she's more likely to wrestle around with you in the sheets.

5. Look at her face a lot. Women love it when guys get so carried away with excitement

WHEN APARTMENTS ATTACK

Hard to believe your humble home could possibly turn against you... but it can. And you won't get a second chance, either, because once a woman's scoped out your nasty habitrail, you're through—even if it looks better the second time, she'll assume that you realized she was previously unimpressed (or grossed out) and gussied your place up just to impress her. If you ever expect her to share your bed, you must exterminate the following things from your home.

Girlie-Man Maintenance Products

"I got freaked out when I found a ton of beauty products in the bathroom. I figured either he was more interested in grooming than I was, or he had lots of female visitors. Sex was out of the question." —Rosalind, 25, business writer, Brooklyn, New York

Frat-Boy Shit

"This guy I was dating was living with four other guys in this rat hole. The place was the most unbelievable dump. There was garbage everywhere, cigarette butts in the toilet, a mattress on the balcony, and stolen McDonald's signs in the kitchen. His roommates were always still sleeping at two in the afternoon, and I never felt like I was welcome there. So I stopped going there—and going out with him."
—Sara, 26, writer, San Francisco

Weapons

"On a third or fourth date a couple of years ago, this guy was making me dinner at his apartment, and I noticed that he had a collection of swords in his bedroom. Scary! Then I went into his bathroom and found one of those girl-in-bikini posters. I thought it was kind of odd for a man in his mid-20s to have a cheesy pinup and it was a big turn-off. It was our last date, despite the fact that he was an awesome cook and brought me flowers." —Didi, 26, marketing manager, New York City

they forget everything—except when they forget her, too. "He doesn't have to hold my gaze, just work his way back up to my face once in a while when we're fooling around—it reassures me that he's not imagining Rebecca Romijn-Stamos," says Diane, 30, a patient advocate in Chicago.

6. Be boyishly impetuous. By doing something sweet and (apparently) spontaneous, she'll have great fodder to talk you up to her friends later...and may feel compelled to be spontaneous with you, too. "I was talking about how much I love wildflowers, and suddenly he pulled the car over into a no-parking zone, ran into the mall, and came back with this huge bouquet of daisies," says Angela, 29, a manager at a travel agency in Rochester, New York. "I felt like I owed him...but in a good way."

7. Remember a meaningless holiday. Right at the beginning of the relationship, while you still remember, take out your driver's license and scribble on the back the day and month you first met. Then plan some kind of small surprise for the one-, two-, or three-month anniversary of that date. Even if she's not keeping track, she'll find it irresistible that you are. "I remember he made a toast 'to our first 30 days together,' implying that he was willing to commit to more days together," says Madison, 29, a writer in San Francisco. "It was reassuring, like we were a team. We ended up toasting ourselves again—at breakfast the next morning!"

8. Work her in public. Walk up behind her at a party and say in her ear, "You're the most beautiful woman here," make goo-goo eyes at her across the room, or slip her a naughty note at a formal function about what you'd like to do later. "Every time he would make eyes at me across the room, it would just build the anticipation," says Blair, 36, a career consultant in Rockford, Illinois. "He had two dozen friends there, yet he was all about me—so later, I was all over him."

Spruce Up
Your Love Shack

The babe of your dreams calls at ten to seven to say she's in the area and wants to "drop by." This isn't as causal as it sounds: Women don't just drop by; they embark on reconnaissance missions, searching your lair for clues that will help them decide whether you're worthy of their triple-X gifts. You've got 10 minutes to make your pad presentable—here's the game plan.

• **6:50 p.m.** Start in the bathroom by breaking out a brand-new roll of TP. (To women, that clean, fresh roll implies regular bathroom maintenance.) Then tear off a strip of about 15 squares, wet it, wad it, and wipe the yellow dribble from the front of the throne. Do a quick swirl both around and inside the rim, flush the evidence, and don't forget to put the seat down.

• **6:51 p.m.** Scoop up all ointments, laxatives, extra toothbrushes, industrial-size condom boxes, and girlie-hygiene products your ex left behind, and bury them somewhere safe. (The medicine cabinet is not safe—she will peek.) Pull the shower curtain closed.

• **6:52 p.m.** Crack the window in the bathroom, then do the same near the garbage and the doggy bowl. To disable her advanced nasal radar, replace the odors with any aroma: a squirt of cleaning liquid, a hint of incense, even a lit and blown-out match.

• **6:53 p.m.** Using a plastic grocery bag, do a flyby, collecting empty food and drink containers along with other items that scream, "Frat house!" Take the bag outside, or at least tie it closed and place it by the back door, as if you were just about to take it outside.

• **6:54 p.m.** Grab all dishes and glasses, and introduce them to the sink. But don't waste valuable time on cleaning: simply fill the sink with hot water and detergent. (Bubbles equal camouflage.)

• **6:56 p.m.** Gather stray clothes, dirty or not, jam them in your closet, and shut the door. (Throw your shoulder into it if you have to.)

Tasteful Nudes

"A guy should never have nudes on the walls (not even Renoirs), because it's just weird, and definitely no pictures of just himself, the apparent narcissist." —Mina, 30, freelance artist, New York City

Substandard Sleeping Arrangements

"I wouldn't sleep with my boyfriend at first because his loft felt like a dorm room, complete with a futon and a giant Jimi Hendrix poster on his bedroom wall. My first impression was: Help!" —Sally, 31, teacher, Ann Arbor, Michigan

Six-Legged Surprises

"My date was an architect, and I went to his house after he told me about his great 'Victorian' place. It ended up being a run-down building with cockroaches crawling up the walls with no charm whatsoever. It would have been a whole lot better if he had told the truth up-front." —Trina, 27, musician, Alameida, California

Juvenile Stuff

"No satin sheets, no cocktail bar, no comic books in plastic wrappers, no neon bar signs, no Patrick Nagel artwork of sexy ladies. To me, it all says, 'I'm a fan of the band Rush, not living in reality, and an adolescent forever.'" —Jamie, 29, social worker, Philadelphia

Bathroom Grime

"The bathroom was so grimy, I was afraid to touch anything or sit down. And then there was no toilet paper. I know guys don't have to use it every time, but women can't just shake it off, OK? I mean, if you can't keep toilet paper stocked, then how organized can the rest of your life be? And what are the chances that you remembered to buy condoms?" —Phoebe, 26, software designer, Seattle

Swamp Gas

"Just the whole guy smell can be a turn-off: stale cologne, gym socks, smoke, sex, pizza, body odor, and rooms that smell like a window has never been opened in them." —Maggie, 23, editorial assistant, Garden City, New York

• **6:57 p.m.** While you're there, lose the sweats. Slap on jeans or khakis and your cleanest, plainest T-shirt. (Years of cheerful Gap ads have conditioned women to trust a man in a plain tee.)

• **6:59 p.m.** Conduct a quick scan of the house for remaining girl-related para-phernalia, including photos, letters, and phone numbers. Even your sister's pic must go—otherwise your hot prospect will be trying to ID the mystery woman at the exact moment you want her to stop thinking altogether.

• **7:00 p.m.** Quickly jot down her phone number and place it on your night table, as if you were just about to call her. Then rotate your favorite takeout menu to the top of the stack—you'll be staying in tonight.

Get Her Over the Hump

Why do women make such a big deal about having sex for the first time with some-one new? After all, if she's done it before, what's the big deal? But to us women, who have a million little sex issues going on inside our heads, each first time is a whole different ball game, with different rules. Here are women's biggest fears, according to *Glamour, Cosmopolitan,* and *New Woman* magazines, plus expert advice from Tracey Cox, author of *Hot Sex: How to Do It,* on how to address her cute li'l concerns and keep the ball rolling.

> SO HE LOOKED UP AT ME, SIGHED, AND STARTED SINGING, 'KUM-BA-YAH, MY LORD, KUM-BA-YAH...' AS HE KISSED MY STOMACH.

Her fear: She doesn't know you well enough to let you see her personal playthings. It's all happening too fast.

Your tactic: Play up the fact that you're her friend, too, and emphasize your out-of-bed ties. Say something like, "I know we haven't known each other that long, but I really feel like we connect." (It sends the same message as—but is a lot less Hollywood cheesy than—"You complete me.")

Her fear: The two of you won't click in the sack.

Your tactic: Don't pull her toward the bedroom too soon. Instead, pretend you're in high school, and run a few bases on the couch. She'll get a preview of how the two of you work together. (Hint: If you can't tell what she likes initially, err on the side of touching her too softly and slowly—it's easier for women to say, "Harder, faster," than the more negative, "No, slower, softer.")

Her fear: She wants you bad but worries you'll think she's slutty.

Your tactic: Oblige her by being the aggressor, so she doesn't have to—but make absolutely sure you're reading her I-want-sex signals correctly. Some classic signals: She holds eye contact while you're kissing, touches you a lot, sits back on the couch and puts her legs in your lap, and doesn't put her clothing back in order when you two come up for air. However, Cox warns, you should still say something requiring an unambiguous response, like, "Do you want to move into the bed-room?" to ensure she's really ready and isn't just a diabolical tease.

Her fear: She'll be too nervous to climax.

Your tactic: Tell her you're a little nervous, too...then calm her down. It's not

uncommon for a woman who has no problem having an orgasm in a continuing relationship to be unable to get there with a new partner. The experts suggest relaxing her by lying together so her breathing and heart rate will slow down to match yours. So if she's the nervous type, just rent a movie and watch it while lying together on the sofa. By the time the credits roll, she'll want to, too!

Her fear: You won't know what she likes.

Your tactic: Put her at ease by saying, "I want to learn what you like." (Hint: Stay away from "Show me what you like," which puts pressure on her.) Or, as you're rounding the initial bases, ask, "Is this too hard?" or "Does this feel good?" so she knows that you'll be open to suggestions when you get to her more complicated motherboard. Also, pay attention to her body language. Rapid breathing and clinging to you mean: "Keep doing that—don't stop!"

Her fear: She'll have to broach the awkward subject of safe sex.

Your tactic: You need a two-pronged strategy. She'll worry twice, once when you're making out and once right before the act. So as you're making out, say, "You're making me so excited—and we don't have to—but if you want to, I'm prepared." She wants to hear the word *prepared* combined with the message that she's in control. Then, when you're suddenly about to have sex, suggests Cox, say, "I'm so turned on, I think we'd better get a condom out now. If we keep going, there's no way we'll want to stop." In other words, don't *suggest* using a condom—take it for granted that you will be.

Her fear: You'll be turned off by her body.

Your tactic: Make sure you compliment her looks while she's still clothed—we women buy clothes to show off our assets but also to camouflage parts we don't like—and at *each stage* of disrobing. (If you gasp and say, "You're so beautiful" when she takes off her bra but not when she steps out of her panties, she'll worry even more.) Once you've expressed your admiration for her body, she'll feel comfortable enough to let you hop on her little love train. All aboard!

Five Things to Do Right After Sex

With sex, it ain't over when it's over...not if you ever want her to come back, that is. This checklist will ensure that the next time you see her she'll be hungry for more.

1. Acknowledge the earth-shaking event that just occurred.
Say something, anything, even just "wow," to show her it was a big deal to you, too.

2. Allude to the next time. It helps ease her fear that now that you've had her, you're outta there. (Or she's outta there, if it's your apartment.) Bonus: Women's complicated plumbing means even if you were a Casanova who made her scream, it's likely the second or third time will be even better.

3. Consider her comfort. Ask her if she's chilly and pull the blankets up over her shoulders, find the cigarettes, get her a glass of water, fetch some Bactine for the carpet burn on her back or knees, etc. Pampering her tells her you weren't just in it for the sex. And that's what you want her to believe, isn't it?

4. Ask her what she wants to do next. If she just wants to sleep, great. But 99.9 percent of the men she's been with have grunted and sunk into instant sex-coma, so you want to imply that the *next* half-hour is as important as the *last* half-hour. Offer to cuddle, change the CD, check who's hosting *SNL,* or see if there's any ice cream left and you'll immediately be catapulted into the category of überlover.

5. Rub, touch, or stroke her body in a sensual but nonsexual way. By doing that, you let her know that you honestly do love her body, in a pure way...it wasn't just the testosterone talking.

Five Things to Do the Following Week

By the time she's given her girlfriends a basic rundown of your gymnastic, drunken, underwear-ripping midnight tryst (about three minutes after you dropped her off), she'll start having questions and concerns. She'll be worried that you didn't have enough fun, or that she was too loud or too quiet or too jiggly, etc. Five small reassurances to dole out over the coming week to let her know you're in for the long haul:

1. Tell her it was amazing and, this is crucial, "I can't stop thinking about it." It reassures her that you've stopped thinking about having sex with your ex forever.

2. Share a small fear, any small fear. It'll make her relieved that you were concerned about pleasing her. "I like it when a guy says, 'I hope I wasn't too quick' or 'I hope it was good for you' because it shows he's sensitive and concerned," says Erica, 28, a day-care worker in Louisville, Kentucky.

3. Give a public display of affection. All her girlfriends know you've done the deed, so you'll get triple points for whatever action you take, whether it's sending flowers to her at work, faxing her a big "Wow," or showing up at her office with a picnic basket.

4. Call her when you say you'll call. After the movie *Swingers*, guys started to think there was a magic number of days to wait. Not so, explains Jessica, 29, a production manager in Boston: "The crucial thing is that he's a man of his word. So whether he says he'll call the next day or two days later when he finishes a project, he needs to make that deadline, because I have it written down in my calendar!"

5. Line up the next date. After a few more go-arounds, you'll be able to get horizontal without wading through the whole dinner/date thing, but she's still in a delicate zone, so plan a nice dinner or night out—something so she knows she wasn't just a one-night wonder girl.

chapter five

Romance Her

Here's how to make dating you a story worth telling her friends.

Why the hell is romance so important to women, anyway? To try to put this in perspective for you, women say they imagine it feels like the giddy thrill of effortlessly getting free playoff tickets combined with the news that there's a new Baywatch *show called* Teeny-Weeny-Bikini Baywatch. *The good news: So many men are so painfully deficient at romance skills that just an adequate showing on your part is enough to make women adore you and want to straddle you in semipublic places. If nothing else, it gives your gal bragging rights during the next round of Chick Comparathon with her cute friends (if you're a forward-thinking kind of guy, you can think of this as planning for the future).*

The downside is that it's a complex, baffling little world in which the only things you know—red roses, boxes of chocolates, candlelit dinners—are so clichéd they're usually worse than doing nothing at all. Yikes! "Women have started to realize that a man who follows all the romantic conventions might just be in love with romance—not with her," says Lillian Glass, author of He Says She Says: Closing the Communication Gap Between the Sexes.

But don't be scared off: It's not impossible to maneuver in this world, and since your competition's essentially two billion Al Bundys, this one blitzkrieg chapter contains everything you need to shine like a diamond in a goat's ass.

New Game Plans for Classic Dates

Movies, dinners, etc., may be boring date options, but that's what you want in the very beginning—boring equals comfort and safety, and provides a bland backdrop against which your personality can sparkle its brightest. After a while, though, it's time to change it up, or she'll be falling asleep in the soup. Here are some easier-to-assemble-than-an-IKEA-bookshelf instructions for twisting an ordinary date into an extraordinary one.

the movie

old plan: Go to theater. Buy tickets. Watch movie in complete silence, as if other person isn't right next to you. Go home. Wonder if she likes you.

new plan:

1. Earlier in the day, stop at Bath & Body Works (or Pier 1 Imports or even the Gap) and buy several nice-smelling candles (vanilla scented is nice and won't make your living room smell like a perfume counter).

2. That night, get takeout from her favorite restaurant, then go to the video store and rent that sappy chick-ish flick you refused to see with her in the theater.

3. Arrange the blankets and pillows in your den, transforming it into The Pamper-Her Zone.

4. Place candles on the coffee table and TV and around the living room area, light them, and turn the rest of the lights off.

5. Put the movie into the VCR and wait for your overjoyed honey to show—and show her appreciation.

the nighttime stroll

old plan: Take a walk nowhere in particular, lend her your sweater for the marginally cooler return trip, turn around and come home. Dream of someday buying a car.

new plan:

1. Casually mention you'd like to take a walk.

2. Steer her in the direction of a memorable place (where you first met, first kissed, first said you loved her—hopefully not all of these are Burger King parking lots).

3. When you get to the spot, turn her toward you and look into her eyes. If she's a little spacey and doesn't get it, say, "Remember this spot?" Grin sheepishly as she throws herself into your arms and squeals with delight because you are so sensitive and cool.

4. If she doesn't throw herself into your arms and squeal with delight, she could be the only nonromantic woman on the planet. This could be good. Take her home and commence nonstop shagging.

the dinner

old plan: Go to restaurant. Eat. Drink. Go home. Burp.

new plan:

1. Buy (or borrow from your female neighbor) some sort of picnic basket. Note: Your Igloo cooler is not a picnic basket; neither is the box your car stereo came in.

2. Go to a grocery store or restaurant and get some sort of takeout food (i.e., sandwiches, pasta salad, fried chicken, and fruit—all women love fruit, and they look so sexy with peach juice dribbling down their chins).

3. Pack the basket with food, utensils (real ones, not plastic), napkins (cloth if you have them), drinks, glasses, a blanket to sit on, and some candles.

4. Bring her to, ideally, a park or beach. But your rooftop, the back of your 4x4 (as long as you park somewhere with a view), or, if it's the middle of winter, even her living room floor will score you points for creativity.

5. Arrange the food and indulge.

dancing

old plan: Go to club. Dance to blaring music while pointing and laughing at the more spastic dancers. Go home and change into nonsweaty clothes.

new plan:

1. Rent a learn-to-tango video. Salsa, meringue, and swing videos also score big points. (Note: Don't grab the wrong type of swing video...that's another kind of date altogether.)

2. Invite her over to hang out—but let the dancing part be a surprise.

3. Move the couch, and breakables, out of the way.

4. Watch the video and try to follow along without trampling her toes. (If you're not *Saturday Night Fever* material, you might want to watch the video once *before* she comes over.)

5. Remember to tell her she's a great dancer. When dancing turns to making out, you know you've got the steps right.

How to Pull Off the Superdate

There's no surer way to a woman's heart than the superdate: a romantic event orchestrated by you that gives her tangible examples of your wonderfulness, which she can show off to the approximately

145 women who will know all the intimate details of this date before your head hits the pillow. She gets to make all her friends jealous; you come out smelling like a rose...everybody wins. For inspiration, we've asked women to share the dates they'll never forget—and distill the critical advice for you so you, too, can give her a night to remember.

SLICING OUT THE CHEESE

There's a fine line between making her all warm and tingly inside and giving her indigestion. Here, let *Maxim*'s CheeseMeter tell you if something is delectably acceptable or a nauseating no-no.

The move: Making a big heart in the bathroom mirror so she'll see it when it steams up.

CheeseMeter says: Velveeta. It's generic and expected—she's processed this one before. Women love to be surprised, but not by Casey Kasem.

Instead, try: Slipping a note into her purse or bag that she'll find later that simply says, "Can't stop thinking about you, [her name here]."

The move: Joking "I think I love you" on the first date.

CheeseMeter says: Brie. Only a Frenchman would try a joke this mushy; she'll now have to question anything you say about her.

Instead, try: "You're unlike any woman I've ever met." It's easier for her to believe, and she'll keep thinking about you all week as she ponders what exactly you meant.

The move: Dedicating a song to her on the radio.

CheeseMeter says: Gorgonzola. This one carries the heady reek of pathetic puppy love.

Instead, try: If you want to make a public display, offer a toast to her at the next gathering with friends, even if it's over beers. Keep it simple: "To Kelly, a priceless beauty I don't deserve...but will gladly accept."

The move: Saying during sex, "Tell me what it feels like—I want to know what it's like to be a woman."

CheeseMeter says: Cheez Whiz. Even heated up with passion, it makes her cringe. One of you is going to have to go into therapy.

Instead, try: "I want to know everything about your body." This conveys the same passionate message but doesn't make her think you're considering switching teams.

"It was cloudy, and I thought my new boyfriend and I were just going to end up sitting on the couch watching *Frasier* reruns. Then he announced out of the blue that he was going to take me to Nantucket, which was a few hours away. We rented a motorbike and went all around the island. The fact that it was bad weather made it that much more fun because it was so crazy and impromptu and romantic. He's usually the predictable one and I'm crazier, so it was great that it was *his* idea. We had dinner and took the last ferry back." —Ellen, 25, intern coordinator, Boston

Tantalize-her tip: If you're doing the same stuff every night (dinner, video, movie, drinks), shake it up by doing something spontaneous (like a mini hiking trip, a boat ride, a long bike ride). If you're not a spontaneous guy, come up with the date idea a week in advance, but spring it on her that afternoon so she'll think you just had a stroke of sweet genius!

"I'd been working a ton and we had been just meeting for quick dinners most nights, when he surprised me by getting tickets for a play at a Victorian opera house in the country that I'd mentioned once. He planned it so that we had time for dinner at a quaint little restaurant, followed by a walk by the river before the play. I'm indecisive, so nothing pleases me more than a guy who thinks enough of me to make the phone calls and plan a great night.

It's all about making me feel special." —Jordan, 37, doctor, Savannah

Tantalize-her tip: Make it a three-course date that involves at least two things that you had to reserve in advance, like tickets on a ferry or seats for a show. It proves to her that you're thinking about her sweet little self even when she's not around.

"I was new to the city and we'd met through work, so I was nervous about being on a date with a virtual stranger. But he chose a very public place with huge windows, which told me that he understood how scary dating can be for a woman in a big, new city. Also, he showed up early to beat the after-work rush so that I would be able to sit down instead of standing at the bar, which showed he was considerate. I felt like a pampered princess because he'd known to do these basic things that the last three guys had been clueless about." —Missy, 24, copy editor, Brooklyn, New York

Tantalize-her tip: Always keep first dates in public places (unless *she* wants to move it to the private sector). You want her to be comfortable, not preoccupied with the idea of finding an escape route should you turn out to be Ted Bundy (or even Al Bundy).

"The one thing that really makes me melt is when a guy cooks for me. It shows he cares because he's doing something that requires preparation and planning. You also get to have a long, slow evening where you can really just enjoy each other's company and not think about where you're going to go for dessert and coffee or a drink. Just make sure she's into you before attempting this, because inviting a woman to your house for a meal is pretty much going to be interpreted as inviting her over for sex. Which is great if the woman wants to have sex, or at least some kind of major make-out session; but if she's still getting to know you, it might flip her out." —Mia, 26, designer, Columbus, Ohio

Tantalize-her tip: If you can't cook, at least master one meal that you can use to impress many babes over time. (This meal's name should not end with "'n Cheese.") Bonus: Handiness in the kitchen will lead her to believe you're willing to pitch in with domestic chores in the future, an illusion it's hardly worth shattering at this early date.

"My best date ever was when my boyfriend-to-be (we'd been out on only two dates) took me to the beach for a picnic. He'd picked up sandwiches and drinks—cans of Coke, nothing fancy—but after we got there he laid out the blanket and put a vase with a pink rose in the middle. It was a small gesture, but it showed that he had put some thought into the date and that he was trying to impress me. Otherwise, it

could have just been like an afternoon at the beach with his buddies; but the rose said he had been conscious of the fact that it was me he was spending the day with." —Irene, 35, freelance researcher, Boston

Tantalize-her tip: A little attention to detail goes a long way—and it's so easy it's laughable.

"This guy took me to a hockey game...no, really! When he asked me I was intrigued because it sounded so different and it was pretty ballsy of him to throw the idea out, considering that hockey isn't traditionally a female favorite. Turns out, he was testing me to see if I was game, which I was. We had a great time drinking beer and eating hot dogs, and I was so happy not to be under pressure at a fancy restaurant." —Wendy, 23, graduate student, New Canaan, Connecticut

Tantalize-her tip: Don't be afraid to try out something you like on her, even if it's a classic guy thing—it's honest and straightforward, and it tells her something about you. Just be prepared to catch a Merchant Ivory flick and do some ballroom dancing when you're on her clock.

The Girlfriend Play: Staking Your Claim ✓

What can you do to make sure she's yours and yours alone? Since keeping her locked in the bedroom is out, you have to make sure she's emotionally locked in. Here, real women tell what catapulted their men from simple crushes to He's-The-One boyfriends—and suggest ways to speed up the process so you can get back to watching the game.

Tactic: Tell her you're *the* man. At some point in every relationship, somebody suggests it's time to start dating exclusively. It's almost always the woman—keep your biological-clock cracks to yourself, bucko—but if you do it, she'll trust your monogamy more (since it was your idea!). The key, women warn, is to deliver this message sweetly, not possessively. "The word *exclusive* is unromantic," says Blair, 36, a career consultant in Rockford, Illinois, "and I don't want a guy laying down rules for me to follow right off the bat."

> SO MANY MEN ARE SO PAINFULLY DEFICIENT AT ROMANCE SKILLS THAT JUST AN ADEQUATE SHOWING ON YOUR PART IS ENOUGH TO MAKE WOMEN ADORE YOU AND WANT TO STRADDLE YOU IN SEMIPUBLIC PLACES.

Fast-forward tip: Don't wait weeks or months to bring up the exclusivity clause. "Just say, 'I like being with you so much, and I don't want to be with anyone else,'" advises Blair. Why it works: Women find this line irresistible because by a certain age all women have been with at least one guy who they thought was being exclusive, only to get burned by the truth that he wasn't. Just don't be the first to market with this: If she's never initiated any kind of relationshippy talk, hold off on this line, no matter how grand her Tetons are. "If he says he wants to be exclusive too soon, he sounds like a dork," says Patti, 23, an advertising associate in Madison, Wisconsin.

Tactic: Leave her hungry. Pulling back a little and not being able to spend all your time with her makes her want you more. Even your taking a trip with the guys can make her fret, cutting the normal boyfriend break-in time in half. "My current boyfriend earned exclusive status because he was going on a ski trip with the guys," says Simone, 30, a writer in Hoboken, New Jersey. "The thought of him sitting in a hot tub with some cute ski bunny made me feel so miserable that I realized he was worth giving up my own nights of flirting." Just don't be too distant—you'll piss off the cuddler variety of babe.

Fast-forward tip: Don't wait for your yearly Vegas pokerfest: The next time she's going away can be just as good an opportunity to push the issue. "I was going on a spring-break trip with some

NEVER, EVER, EVER GIVE HER...

The Wonderbra

Ponds Hand Cream

An exercise bike

A gift basket of assorted cleaning supplies

Six-foot, 200-watts-per-channel wall speakers

Enrollment at the local Oral Sex Academy

Dinner for two at Hooters

A year's supply of Jenny Craig meals

A secretly taped video of you and her having passionate sex, with humorous commentary

Golf lessons

A gift certificate for a tummy tuck

The Guide to Better Sex video

The Epilady hair-removal system

Clairol blonde hair dye

Cash

girlfriends, and he said, 'Hey, you better not let any Mexican boys see your special mole,'" says Paige, 24, a nursing student in Houston, Texas. "He was talking about the mole I have next to my left nipple. He said it in such a cute, playful way that there wasn't any pressure, but it still got the message across—I was his girl now."

Tactic: Invite her to a family function. To women, this practically proves you're exclusive. Why? Because they'll give you the benefit of the doubt and assume you wouldn't show up at weddings, reunions, or family birthdays with a flavor of the month for each event. "If I invite a guy to a wedding or a family function, that means he's more than just a date, and I assume it's the same with him," says Michele, 22, a design student in Providence.

Fast-forward tip: If your family reunion's 11 months away, create an ersatz family event. Your brother and his wife owe you for letting them use your time-share? Remind them you're still waiting for your dinner...then stretch the invite to plus-one and bring along your babe. Any blood relative (or anyone you can pay to be your blood relative and talk you up) will do. Also, whenever she's on the phone with her family or friends, say, "Tell them I say hello." It fast-forwards your connections in her world, and she'll start to think of you as an integrated part of it.

Tactic: Go on a "nondate" with her. "You know he's your boyfriend when he's willing to do nondate stuff together, like sanding a table or helping you finish your Web page," says Jaqueline, 30, an illustrator in San Diego. It also helps you seem less like a single-minded sex pervert. (Unless you link her Web page to 200 porn sites...)

Fast-forward tip: You'll seem just as attractively innocent if you offer to combine errands with her or join her in a shopping excursion for random stuff at Kmart—stuff that women, efficient list-making creatures that they are, do every week. It sends the same message: You like to be with her all the time, and not just in bed. And as long as you're not too Alan Alda about it, she'll appreciate it...and show her appreciation by bedding you. We're so sweet, aren't we?

Romance Gone Wrong!

Straight from the fillies' mouths, here are some examples of classic romantic blunders. Read these anecdotes or become one.

"I could tell this guy wanted to impress me, so he took me to a *really* fancy restaurant and said he wanted it to be a special night. The problem was, when I asked if he'd been there before he said yes, but it became obvious he hadn't. He hadn't realized the dress code called for a jacket, and he didn't know where the rest rooms were. I spent the rest of the evening wondering what other baloney he was feeding me." —Ann, 26, social worker, Fairfield, Connecticut

"Every day the week before Valentine's Day, he sent me a different one of those candy hearts with a message—'Be Mine,' or whatever. Cute, but then he seriously denied it was him, even though the printing on the envelope was so obviously his.

One minute you're talking about Ultimate Frisbee and the next she's telling you how her mother's responsible for killing her ambition. What the hell happened? Well, women, fueled by the likes of Oprah, Ricki, and Jerry, feel that one of the best ways to bond with you is to spill their guts—and they expect you to listen with the skill of a shrink. (But they refuse to pay you—don't even ask, it's a land mine.) But never fear: Here's how to be her personal baggage handler.

LISTENING MADE EASY

1 Let her get it all out. Nod knowingly. When she says, "I'm probably boring you," disagree and prod her to keep sharing. (Get it over with now; otherwise, she'll just bring it up the next time she's drunk—alcohol often prompts these "couch sessions.")

2 When her jaw stops moving up and down, ask these two questions: "How do you feel about it now?" and then, "Is there anything I can do?" The first will give you the synopsis you need to remember this discussion later and will do your analysis for you so you'll know what to do. (Example: If she says, "I guess what it all boils down to is that I still feel like that junior high ugly duckling," reassure her all week how gorgeous she is.) The second will earn you points for being protective and concerned, and yet you won't have to do anything

I was like, 'OK, sneaky, right, it's not you.' How dumb did he think I was?" —Tanya, 19, waitress/artist, Pittsburgh

"I told him I loved amusement parks, so he surprised me with a trip to the nearest one. Unfortunately his sister had an emergency and needed a baby-sitter. But instead of canceling, he brought five-year-old Sammy with us. I love kids, but I spent our 'romantic' day at Worlds of Fun listening to the pipsqueak yell, 'Kissing is gross!' every time we even held hands." —Cindy, 25, a social worker in Bronx, New York

beyond the listening you've already done.

3 Follow up by saying, "You know you can always talk to me about anything." At this point you're off the hook if her talk-show topic was something you couldn't possibly relate to (getting third runner-up for prom queen, or a serious chick issue like an eating disorder). But if she was hung up on a universal theme (feeling distant from the folks), then she'll expect you to chime in a little, so proceed to step 3a.

3a Share a brief, painful story. Example: You broke your leg right before the season started and had to watch your best friend take over your position, and it made it hard to remain buddies because you were so jealous, even though you knew you were being petty, the end. It's a sure bet the other guys she's known were too scared or intimidated to share after her scary sharing time, so any little ditty you can come up with will score big bonding points.

4 Congratulate yourself. You have survived sharing time, bought yourself at least a month before her next urge to emotionally purge, and she's now a sappy mess in need of another type of on-the-couch action. (Step #1: "I feel like I just have to hold you...")

"He secretly decorated my car on my birthday with streamers and tied cans to my bumper. All my neighbors thought I'd just gotten married. Then he left me to clean it all off!" —Beth, 21, property management assistant, Des Moines, Iowa

"For my homecoming—I'd been away traveling for a month—he suggested we go to the same restaurant and bars that we did on our first date. I was floored that he *remembered* the details of our first date. What could go wrong? Well, he told all of our friends where we would be. Our 'romantic homecoming' turned into a date for 12. At the end of the date, I told him I was too tired to sleep over." —Brenda, 26, business consultant, Chicago

"For our six-month anniversary, he had matching T-shirts made for us that read, 'Six months and counting.' I felt like I was part of some fraternity theme party. The shirt is now at Goodwill." —Helen, 28, cooking student, New York City

The Massage Technique Her Ex Didn't Know

Want to give a woman what she *really* wants? Then give her a massage that *isn't* just a back-door way to get her to take off her bra and whisk her into bed. Sure, the pampering and the physical enjoyment make massages so pleasurable for us women that it always works as fast-forward foreplay. But that's what we've come to expect from men now, and you can score major points by giving it to us without strings attached. "She'll enjoy her massage more if it's just a pleasurable experience in itself and not a pressured invitation to sex," explains Gordon Inkeles, author of the book *The New Sensual Massage* (Arcata Arts, 1998), who also leads massage workshops.

To help you focus on her pleasure (don't worry, brownie points can still be redeemed for sex down the line), here's a great new technique called "spot friction" that'll make her melt into a quivering mass.

First, don't jump the gun. If you've already slept together, then all systems are go for a full-body massage. But if you haven't shared sheets in the biblical sense, your offer to trail your hands all over her naked body will sound unduly lecherous— limit your magic fingers to her neck and shoulder area. Which isn't a bad place to start anyway: A woman's neck and shoulders are a lot smaller than yours, but her head is almost the same size, so her shoulders and neck are working much harder to support that sweet little noggin. (Men, in contrast, hold most of their tension in their lower backs.)

Next, grab some lube. Massage oil or lotion isn't necessary for a soothing massage, but lubricating the skin will let you manipulate the muscles without stretching the skin painfully, and some women say it makes the experience more erotic.

Let your fingers do the walking. First, though, ask if she has any specific aches. Ninety-nine percent of the time she will; if so, start there. The technique's a basic rubbing movement that will feel great anywhere on her back. Make a lobster claw out of your nondominant hand, pushing your thumb and your pressed-together fingers down a few inches on either side of your target spot. (This is called your "anchor hand.") Squeeze the loose flesh together, raising a little hill of flesh between your thumb and your fingers. (You shouldn't be touching the sore spot with your anchor hand—just raising the flesh around it.) Finally, keeping your anchor hand anchored, press down on the sore spot itself with all four fingers of your other hand, circling slowly while pressing down. Be careful not to pull her skin too far while you circle, or else it'll feel like you're pinching her. Repeat, moving your hands slowly across her shoulders and upper back in a methodical way (don't skip from one area of her back to another—it's not as relaxing). Drive all tension from her body; bask in a whatta-guy glow.

FIVE TIPS TO MAKE GIFT BUYING EASIER

We know you hate to shop, and we're guessing part of the reason is that you don't know the tricks of the trade. Here's the inside scoop on shopping for a woman.

Tip #1: Get a personal shopper.
Surprise! If you call ahead to stores of the Saks-Bloomingdale's-Nordstrom ilk, they'll set you up with a personal shopper, i.e. a supersmart shopping slave whose job it is to make sure you leave the store with a perfect gift. And it usually costs nothing!

Tip #2: Bring a photo.
A good salesperson can glean crucial info from a recently snapped full-body color photo, such as her size and body type (which improve the chances of a perfect fit), and her precise hair, skin, and eye color (which will ensure that the clothes look good on her).

Tip #3: Know what she reads.
Her catalogs provide key data on the look she aspires to, as do her fashion mags. The saleswoman will know how to decode these titles.

Tip #4: Do some closet reconnaissance.
She knows what looks best on her, so pop into her closet and make a list. Write down sizes, colors, labels, and lengths, all of which will help the salesperson. Focus on the front of the closet—the back's where she hides the stuff her mom gave her that she hates. Check her bra size, too: Comparing her breasts to various melons may not endear you to the female salesclerk.

Tip #5: Make strategic errors.
If you don't know the right size to buy, make damned sure you err on the small side! (Bonus: She'll quietly exchange it herself when you're not looking.) And always, always save the receipt: That way she can undo any mistakes you've made...and if you're a very good boy, there's always a chance she'll swap it for lingerie.

> IF YOU CAN'T COOK, AT LEAST MASTER ONE MEAL THAT YOU CAN USE TO IMPRESS MANY BABES OVER TIME (THIS MEAL'S NAME SHOULD NOT END WITH "N CHEESE").

Master the Key to Her Heart: Her Feet

Remember in the beginning of *Pulp Fiction* when John Travolta and Samuel L. Jackson are talking about a man who got killed for giving a foot massage to the boss' wife? Foot massage is one of the most enjoyable, sensual, erotic sensations a woman can have. "When a guy rubs your feet, it's like he's worshiping you," explains Carol, 32, an advertising executive in Houston, Texas. If you don't understand, it's probably because men's shoes fit, whereas we feel compelled to squeeze our feet into ridiculous shoes that bruise and hack our feet to ribbons. Humph.

So here's the game plan: It's simple, it makes her moan, and afterward she'll be too weak to resist your "Wednesday Is Steak Night" idea.

Get her set up. She should be sitting with her back supported or lying face-up, feet naked, the Lifetime channel on the tube. (Think about it: How much better would a blow job be if you could watch *SportsCenter* in the background?) Flowery girl lotion is a nice touch: Odds are she's got some, so just ask her.

Start slowly. Get her relaxed by gently rubbing and squeezing all parts of her feet—using lotion if you've got it, warming up her foot with friction if you don't. Wrap one hand around the ball of her foot and squeeze firmly as if trying to introduce her big and little toes; release, then squeeze again. Cup her heel and squeeze again; rub the skin back and forth across the heel bone. Repeat with foot #2.

Concentrate on her arches. They bear more weight than any other part of her body and are badly abused by high heels and such. Hold the top of her foot with one hand while you press down into the arch with the flat part of your knuckles. Make small circles with your knuckles, and don't be afraid to press down hard—the arch was created to take a lot of pressure, so too light a touch won't feel as moan-worthy to her. If she draws attention to a particular spot ("Ooh, yeah, right there"), you can get more point pressure by using an actual knuckle (instead of the flat part); but be careful: A little goes a long way.

Do the tootsie roll. Take each toe in turn between your thumb and index or middle finger. Tug it gently as if trying to coax it out of the foot, hold it, then twist it gently—clockwise until it stops, then counterclockwise, then back. If she's really tense, you'll hear the crack of tiny little toe knuckles. Isn't she cute?

Go a few feet further. Foot tension can also derive from the muscles of the leg, so finish her off by squeezing and pulling her calf muscles, and work your way up to her thighs. If you hit a panty line, you've gone too far—back up.

The Perfect Gift Every Time

Gifts for girlfriends are always loaded with meaning, whether you want them to be or not. To the female mind, any present you give her is a snapshot of exactly how you feel about her at this point in your relationship. And you can't just throw money at

the problem, because spending big bucks on the wrong thing can backfire worse than no present at all. That's right: worse than no present at all.

Take the example of Ruth, a 29-year-old new-media executive in New York City. Her boyfriend of six months bought her an expensive sweater at classy clothier Barneys New York, and she freaked out. Why? Because even though it was beautiful, she felt weird telling her family and friends that the man she was considering becoming engaged to had bought her an item of clothing as a symbol of his love. As every woman—but no man— knows, a sweater, regardless of price, is a gift you give one to three months into a relationship. Not before, not after.

Ruth explained this to him, they returned the sweater for the appropriate ruby earrings, and everyone lived happily ever after. Now, if he'd bought her the ruby earrings after two months of dating, she'd have felt like he'd just handcuffed himself to her. How the hell do women expect you to navigate this mine field? Answer: We don't. It's a test of your overall romanticism, and to facilitate comparing boyfriends, women designed it to be so tough that no man can get 100 percent. But we're going to help you cheat.

> **FOOT MASSAGE IS ONE OF THE MOST ENJOYABLE, SENSUAL, EROTIC SENSATIONS A WOMAN CAN HAVE.**

If you've been dating...
One month: Watch for her hints.

She's well aware that only a borderline stalker would know her well enough at this phase to sniff out the perfect present, so just pay attention. She'll drop major hints—and if you weren't paying attention, just ask her girlfriends, who'll dish up great ideas and shoulder the blame if they're wrong. (Yes, she'll find out about your snooping, but at this early phase it'll be read as a sincere desire to please her.) Warning: If you've let it go to within three days of the event, it's too late to ask her friends. You'll look like you're not taking their friend seriously enough, and they'll punish you by steering you wrong. ("Emily? All she wants is a pair of edible panties

BUY HER A GIFT WITHOUT LEAVING THE COUCH

You can't buy your gal a gift without lifting a finger. But you might get away with only lifting one, because all the great gifts below are right at your telephone-dialing fingertip. Here's the La-Z-Boy gift guide: Your gal will never be so happy you did so little.

SpaWish gift certificates: It's a nationwide chain that sells gift certificates to spas in your local area. You don't even have to know exactly what goes on at one...just trust us, it's a great idea. Sessions start at $35, but you really should shell out about $100. To order, wait until she's out shopping for you, then call 888-SPA-WISH or check out www.spawish.com.

Tickets to her favorite show: Ticketmaster has everything from Jewel concerts to touring Broadway shows. Call 411 for your local Ticketmaster number, or check out www.telecharge.com.

A gift from Tiffany & Co.: Every woman has had at least one vivid dream of receiving one of its trademark little light blue boxes. And a gift from T&C doesn't have to break your bank, with bracelets and earrings starting between $50 and $85. Call 800-526-0649.

More wine every month: For less than $40 a month, The California Wine Club's Wines of the Month program will send your woman two bottles every 30 days, so she'll be bombed and beholden at least once a month. Call 800-777-4443, or check out www.cawineclub.com.

A monthly potted flower: Ones from Marlborough Green Houses will run you a total of around $100, depending on which type of flowers and how many months you want them delivered. Call 603-876-4397, or go to www.marlboroughgreenhouses.com.

and a bullwhip.") But don't panic—any of these will do in a pinch: a dozen tulips, a little silver or ceramic box or container, a simple black or white sweater ($50–$100, no more), a flower or bud vase, dinner at a restaurant she knows you can't quite afford, a CD that you know she loves and doesn't have, a delicate teapot if she drinks tea.

Three months: Gift certificate with a flower chaser.

Gift certificates are still safe here; at six months she'll find it too impersonal. We're talking chick products and services, and you ought to know her well enough by now to know what kind of goods and services will float her boat. (Bad bets: McDonald's, Ace Hardware. Good bets: day spas, massages, her favorite clothing or garden store.) Use the card to put the gift certificate in the context of your shared experience and that'll personalize it enough to make her adore you. Add a single flower and you're golden.

Six months: Something sparkly.

Congratulations (or condolences): You have now entered the jewelry zone. Stay away from 1) diamond earrings and 2) any type of ring unless you're already thinking marriage, because that's what they make *her* think of. Safer but just as precious are bracelets, nondiamond earrings, and necklaces. As to style, individuals vary widely, and you should pay attention to what she already wears. But if in doubt, it's safest to lean toward something more delicate than clunky. If the jewelry counter freaks you out, get her: a gorgeous, hand-embroidered handbag; a vintage, early edition hardback of a book she loves; a small, beautifully framed mirror to hang on her wall; or a silk scarf or leather gloves from a fancy department store.

One year: Something fabulous and meaningful.

You've been dating for a while now, and she'll expect you to know her pretty well, so try to

Score Me

Keep in mind that while "you have a great body" is sweet, specifics resonate more in her blissed-out little head. (page 167)

Win Me

So many men are so painfully deficient at romance skills that just an adequate showing on your part is enough to make women adore you and want to straddle you in semi-public places. (page 83)

Seduce Me

Try looking into her eyes in bed: Since you could be ogling her nudity, but are opting instead to look into the windows of her soul, she'll know you're crazy about her, in every sense. (page 169)

Catch Me

Women love men who can roll out the laughs and keep them giggling—a talent that can make up for a million physical shortcomings. (page 37)

Score Me

Don't use the word "baby." Unless you're a legitimate Hollywood director, you might as well drive up with a "Pedophiles R Us" bumper sticker. (page 34)

Thrill Me

The good news, according to the pros at the Kinsey Institute, is that there is a 50 percent chance that the woman you're with may quite sincerely be interested in someday inviting a friend along for the ride. (page 179)

Figure Me Out
Saying "show me what you like" puts pressure on her, but saying "I want to learn what you like" will put her at ease. (page 77)

Drive Me Wild

Women love requests to wear certain articles of clothing. If there's a bathrobe or some special underwear you say is really sexy, it's sexy for her to wear it for you. (page 170)

Win Me

Try saying, "You're unlike any woman I've ever met." It's easier for her to believe than "I love you" and she'll keep thinking about you all week as she ponders what exactly you meant. (page 86)

Romance Me

Women's brains are hardwired so that they're incapable of forgetting even the tiniest little damn nitpicky thing. So make the most of her Kodak-perfect memory and go do something nice. (page 144)

Score Me

Walk up behind her at a party
and say in her ear, "You're the
most beautiful woman here,"
or slip her a naughty note at
a formal function about what
you'd like to do later. (page 74)

Drive Me Wild

When your gal does something unexpectedly wild or hilarious or amazing, say something. You'll score more points than you ever thought possible. (page 129)

Catch Our Eye

It's easy to assume that a guy who waltzes up and lays a line on a woman will turn her off, but women say that isn't so. When it comes to the modern mating dance, women enjoy being passive and want you to be aggressive. (page 33)

remember her reaction to the previous gifts you gave her: If she loved the handbag but hated the jewelry, get thee to a leather store. Keep in mind that you have to keep upping the ante: You can't give her a gold necklace at six months, then shrink back to a set of teacups at one year, or she'll assume you're on your way out the door. If in doubt, try these one-year whoppers: a weekend away (wrap up the plane tickets or hotel brochure so she has something to rip open); jewelry with a sweet message or both your initials engraved in it (to women, this is a completely different gift than noninscribed jewelry); that gorgeous leather coat she couldn't stop mentioning; or, if you're already playing house with her, a piece of furniture that matches her taste (an antique chest or a tiny dressing table) and says to her, "I love living with you, baby."

Other tips:

- **Personal is always better than generic:** You get extra-credit points for showing you know her and her sense of style (and, where appropriate, her sense of humor).
- **How much should you spend on a birthday or holiday?** Divide your yearly salary (before taxes, cheapskate) by 1,000—that's how much you should spend for every six months you've been dating. So a guy who makes $35,000 and has been dating the girl for 18 months should spend $35 x 3, or $105 ($50 minimum, $200 maximum).
- **How fancy should you go?** Take your cue from her gifts to you: If she bought you a classic watch or conservative tie for your birthday, you'd best take that blender/margarita mix combo back to the store.
- **Quirky, humorous, or homemade gifts**—a mix tape you made just for her, a picture of the two of you in a nice frame—will hit you a big home run in between holidays, when you're picking up bonus points just for giving her a gift for no reason. But for birthdays, anniversaries, etc., when all of her friends are going to call, panting, "What did he give you, huh, huh?" stick with the real stuff.

How to Sign the Card

When we read your cards, we're barely skimming over what the Hallmark minimum-wage copywriter scripted and jumping straight to whatever you wrote. Why? Because how you sign the card, like everything else in your devil-may-care approach to this relationship of ours, gives us massive clues as to how you feel about us. The crucial thing is not to waste the opportunity by using no term of endearment and just scrawling your name. You may as well address the envelope: "To Whom It May Concern."

UNDERSTAND SHE'S GOING TO SCRUTINIZE WHAT YOU WRITE AND TAKE IT VERY SERIOUSLY.

But it's dangerous to dive in with "Love, Joe" too soon, too—because you can never go back. "Understand that she's going to scrutinize what you write and take it very seriously. Every time you up the ante from 'Yours truly' to 'Love' to 'Love always,' it's going to be tougher to cut back, which will be interpreted as you pulling away," points out Dr. Goulston, the couples counselor for iVillage.com. "It's much easier to add more intimacy than it is to take it away."

The easiest trick for pacing your emotional rollout is to hang on to cards she sends you and mimic her closing words: If she says, "xo, Jane," you say, "xo, Joe." Always call, never raise—e.g., "xoxo, Joe"—unless you're damn sure you mean it. And when you get around to the L word, don't toy with us: It's all or nothing. "Luv" or a picture of a heart are cutesy cop-outs she can see right through. If you're not ready to commit to the L word, use other affectionate words, advises Dr. Goulston, such as those x's and o's, or "Hugs and kisses," or "Missing you." If you are ready to commit to the L word, you can still ease into it in stages: "Love," "Much love," "Love always," "All my love," and, finally, the big daddy, "I love you."

Should you include a personal note? Yes, and how much you write should increase with time, so you can show her that as your relationship progresses, even the best cards you can find keep coming up shorter and shorter of trying to explain the powerful emotions she stirs in you. Figure on approximately one original sentence for every three months you've been dating; after a year you should max out and fill that horribly white blank expanse on the inside left of the card. You don't have to, of course, but anything less will be a disappointment—"You and I have been dating for four years, but what luck: This anonymous Hallmark guy pretty much captured exactly how I feel about you!"

A final note: Do a rough draft—you don't need her finding out you whited out "I love you" and replaced it with "Regards." Take a piece of scrap paper and write what you think you wanna write, then wait a day and look it over. Do you come off sounding too cold or too love buggy? Try again. (But hurry—since you're a guy, we're guessing you didn't get this card much in advance of that special day.)

Seven Steps to Getting Her into Sexy Lingerie

Lingerie sounds like the perfect gift, because it makes her feel sexy and it works for you, too. But it ain't as easy as it looks. If any gift tells a girlfriend how you feel about the relationship, an intimate gift tells her how you feel about her sexually. One misstep and she'll think you think she's 1) fat, 2) frumpy, 3) a two-dollar whore straight out of the Old West, or 4) *really* fat. Here's the no-fail strategy for buying her lingerie without a slip. (Er...sorry.)

1. Hit a specialty store. They may be pricier, but you'll get more assistance at a small shop in the mall than at Macy's or from a phone operator from a catalog.

2. Don't ballpark her sizes. Get a pencil and paper, and sneak a look at her bra and panty tags. (Not on her body, you lech—in her drawers.) If you forget or don't get a chance, don't despair. "With just her dress size, height, and weight," says Monica Mitro, a Victoria's Secret spokesperson, "you can still buy a beautiful silk slip and a matching robe."

3. Paint a verbal picture. Talk! Tell the salesperson what sorts of undergarments you've seen your gal wear, and whether she just gave birth or thinks she has the butt of a beluga whale. The more you nail down her tastes and her body anxieties, the more you'll nail...well, the more likely she'll wear your gift more than once.

4. Spring for opulent material. If it feels scratchy or rough in your hands, don't slap it on her tender nether regions—she'll resent your cheapness. Josie Natori, owner of the New York–based Natori lingerie company, suggests you "choose something more special than what she buys for herself." Even if she wears a full-length cotton nightgown to bed, upgrade her to a silk version.

5. Beware the teddy. A one-piece item may look simple and structurally impressive. But if it isn't comfortably stretchy or adjustable, it may not fit the torso of a taller or shorter woman. Let her pick these out on her own.

6. Stick to solid, classic colors. You can't really go wrong here: Better you should look slightly conservative than slightly tacky. "Cream, black, and neutrals are best," says Mitro. "Florals, patterns, and animal prints are riskier." Grrrowwr!

7. No butt floss. Thongs send a sexual, not sexy, message. Even if she owns her share of 'em, odds are she wears 'em for everyday no-panty-line convenience—not because she's dying to flash bare ass at you while mixing midnight margaritas.

chapter six

Figure Her Out

The last unsolved mystery of our time: What the frig *is up with your girl-friend? Here's help.*

So you wined her and dined her, got her horizontal, made her your regular squeeze, and even got her to do that thing with the rubber gloves, the chocolate sauce, and the nurse's outfit. Life with your little lady is one sprawling pleasure zone, isn't it?

And then your favorite golf shirts start disappearing, never to be seen again. Waterloo-level battles erupt over stupid trivialities. She bursts into tears during an AT&T ad. And every couple of weeks, another extra pillow finds its way onto your bed.

What the hell's going through our pretty little heads? Well, it's complicated. If we women had to boil our multiphase madness down to a few simple rules, it'd probably go something like this:

1. There's no problem too mundane to saddle with an emotional component. Everything means something.

2. A conversation ideally should go on until both parties' dried and blistered tongues are so swollen they present a choking hazard (the discussion can then be finished on the phone later). And...

3. Guys will spend their adult lives trying to fill their houses and cars with the biggest speakers they can afford to drown all this out.

Really, women aren't that much more complicated than men; we just operate by a few different principles. And the rewards, because most guys won't make the tiniest effort to figure us out, can be colossal. (Do you have any idea what the reward for surprising her with a day of shopping is? If you don't, you'll be eternally grateful to us when you find out.)

Ready to try to grasp the inner workings of her mind? To wipe that sad-sack 'Now what's she mad about?' look off your face forever? Beware...the journey's not for the timid. The stories, anecdotes, and confessions in the chapter that follows are real: If you have a weak heart, are on medication for panic attacks, or had to fast forward through more than five minutes of Faces of Death, *just skip this chapter. Sissy boy.*

How To Justify Piggy Male Behavior

So your gal wants you to change, to be more sensitive and neat, to stop nodding your head up and down during the opening shots of *Baywatch*? Of course she does: Women call this *training*. "I can tell right away whether a guy has had a serious girl-friend in the past and if she's trained him," explains Sunny, 28, a travel agent in Boston. "If he knows to clean out the drain catcher in the sink and to call when he's supposed to, those are good signs that another woman has done the heavy lifting for me."

Now, a little civilization never hurt anybody. But if you're afraid she wants to make a ballroom-dancin', mineral-water-swillin' Modern Man out of you, a little knowledge of evolutionary biology can help you construct handy scientific excuses for any loutish behavior. Here's how it works.

Her complaint: You're afraid to ask for directions.

Your explanation: Your behavior is easily traceable to the sexes' primordial agendas, according to Deborah Tannen, Ph.D., a linguistics expert and the author of *You Just Don't Understand* (Ballantine Books, 1991). He who seeks status in a hierar-chical society (and you know who you are) is likely to view another who possesses knowledge he himself doesn't as holding a superior position. So the status seeker avoids admitting he's clueless by convincing himself that a third party—even one with a map—would provide the wrong directions. Women know that this is all very silly.

Her complaint: You're never up for a good romance movie.

Your explanation: The male preference for action over emotional drama is

WHAT'S THE BIG DEAL ABOUT WEDDINGS?

Don't blame your girlfriend for her inexplicable wedding fever. She's not putting the pressure on herself to get hitched—she truly does love arranging the furniture any way she pleases and being able to boycott the Super Bowl and watch *Masterpiece Theatre* on her very own TV. No, wedding fever is some-thing you catch from your girlfriends, your family, and from impure contact with those gigantic bridal magazines that grand-mothers anonymously subscribe you to.

Want to keep her in girlfriend status for a few more years before she starts signing checks for God knows what with your last name? Your plan for buying time without losing her entirely starts with peeking inside the marriage-mania pressure cooker. Here's what's cooking in there...and how to keep it stewing for a while.

What she wants: The public declaration of love.

It all boils down to that moment, when the reverend signals for the bride and groom to turn and face their guests, saying, "I now present Mr. and Mrs. Joe Schmo." The man she loves is declaring his love and commit-ment onstage, right in front of everyone else she's ever cared about.

Postpone her with: Suggesting a major public-togetherness action, such as sending out joint Christmas cards, or throwing a dinner party with real invitations that say, "Mike and Carol invite you to..." Alternatively, you could try a big sappy toast in front of all your friends at your local bar...but get a few drinks in you first, so you can pass it off as drunken tomfoolery to your aghast buddies. **Estimated delay:** Four months

What she wants: The big formal party.

If she has two X chromosomes, the itch to plan and pull off a big fat wed-ding has grown unbearable. Her married friends have all had this once-in-a-lifetime chance to liaise with florists, book halls, and plan a menu (yes, women love this fancy-schmancy tedium), and she's dying for a crack at

innate, linked again to the space- and object-oriented hunter's brain. According to anthropologist Helen Fisher in *Anatomy of Love,* voyeuristic activities that engage the eye rather than the emotions (example: football games, titty bars) compare on a primal level with sitting behind a bush in the African veld, trying to decide which route the wildebeests will take. Out of woman's early sensitivity to language arises the tendency to view human drama as high entertainment. (Yeah, we know you like sports bloopers...it ain't the same thing.)

Her complaint: You're trigger-happy with the remote control.

Your explanation: This scenario offers a prime example of the object-happy male brain at work. "Men's brains, which are badly equipped for navigating rocky emotional terrain, revel in the abstract," explains therapist Michael Gurian, author of *The Wonder of Boys* (JP Tarcher, 1997). "The only thing better than the visual stimulation of a TV program is the remote-control-generated riot

being the mostest hostess herself.

Postpone her with: Be on the lookout for party-planning opportunities: your parents' retirement, your sister's wedding shower, etc. If you're at a loss, hint that you've always wanted one of those giant surprise birthday bashes, baby! **Estimated delay:** Six months

What she wants: To get on the baby track.

Now her friends are not only married, they're breeding. She loves her 25-inch waist just the way it is for now, but she is jealous that her gal pals are getting unconditional love from a cute little creature.

Postpone her with: An adorable puppy or kitty. The beast's inherent cuteitude will satiate her motherly instincts, and if you're the one buying it for her, it sends the message "I'm willing to nurture a living, breathing entity with you." **Estimated delay:** Six to eight months

What she wants: The rock.

Think back a minute: What's the nicest piece of jewelry you've ever bought your gal? Was it the $65 birthstone earrings? The $125 teeny opal or cameo on a gold chain? Chump change, pal: If she's going to walk amongst other women, she wants a floodlight on her finger, because foolhardiness on a grand scale ("Yes, m'sieur, eet is a teeny rock, as you say, but it is $3,500 plus zee setting") is the absolute hallmark of true romance.

Postpone her with: Diamond earrings. Something glittery to flash the gals, the set of double solitaires is the universal signal to women that she should stick it out for another 12 months exactly. Two important caveats: First, give 'em to her in a darling velvet box, because that's how she's imagined it in her dreams...but not a ring-shaped box, or she'll think you're fucking with her. (Seriously: Tell the jeweler you want a different-shaped box, and the deal's off if she won't cough one up.) Second, be prepared to propose or move out within a year—those are the chivalrous choices. **Estimated delay:** 12 months of images and objects moving quickly through virtual space. What's actually going on with those objects is beside the point." So when she complains that you don't even know what show you're clicking past, just tell her your DNA made you do it.

Her complaint: You don't pay enough attention to her at parties.

Your explanation: The male tendency to duck one-on-one contact in favor of large-group activity is deeply rooted in evolution, according to Gurian. Career choices were well-defined in prehistoric times: Females cared for children, built communities, and gathered nesting material; men hunted for food. These divisions of labor influenced the ways the brains of men and women evolved: Cavewoman relied on the brain's left side, the side of language skills and emotional reasoning, crucial for nurturing human beings. Caveman depended on right-side gray matter, which controls physical activity and calculates spatial relationships. Tell her you aren't scoping the crowd for other chicks—you're on the lookout for predators.

> **THE MALE PREFERENCE FOR ACTION OVER EMOTIONAL DRAMA IS INNATE, LINKED TO THE SPACE- AND OBJECT-ORIENTED HUNTER'S BRAIN.**

Her complaint: When you get sick, you become completely helpless.

Your explanation: Women, Gurian says, have an uncanny ability to carry on in the face of inconvenience—physical or otherwise—because they are able to process layers of conflicting information in their everyday lives. Men, "who are fueled by aggression-inducing testosterone and wired for compartmentalized thinking," greet obstacles with a far more dramatic reaction. So if you're complaining and she snaps at you, saying, "Oh, be a man about it," the correct response is: "I *am*."

Her complaint: You can't handle mechanical failures.

Your explanation: Research suggests that the male brain turns on like a machine, does its task, then switches off; the female brain is always on. (You're a delivery truck; she's a Denny's.) When you've got a task to complete, there must be no interruptions, no mealy-mouthed guff about printing cartridges. This task orientation is a primary reason why men, during scientific testing, prove less adept than women at performing a number of activities at once. Top off those complications with a little war-making testosterone, and who can blame you if you have a little tantrum every now and then?

Her complaint: You never want to talk.

Your explanation: Guys don't warm as quickly to talking for talking's sake because they're imprinted to value independence; they talk to convey information, and that's all. But a wife or girlfriend can view your lack of interest in yapping as an attempt to avoid bonding with her—a personal rejection if ever there was one. At the heart of women's endless talk about feelings, says linguist Tannen, lurks the essential feminine desire for intimacy. For men, talking just scares all the fish away.

Her complaint: You're unbelievably shallow.

Your explanation: The noncerebral qualities men regard as attractive—a supple body, lustrous hair, youth itself—are all indicative of fertility, a magnet to men on a mission to fulfill their biological imperative to procreate, says anthropologist Fisher. Women, designed to care for the resulting creation, are genetically drawn to guys who can supply a means of sustenance. The good news for you is that the perfectly average-looking schlub—if he can manage to convey that he's a quality schlub with some earning potential—stands a far better chance of waltzing off with a superbabe than, say, a lumpy but golden-hearted woman does of snagging a budding Brad Pitt.

Her complaint: You hate to cuddle after sex.

Your explanation: No, she's not nuts; female brains are just programmed to yearn for sex as an all-inclusive experience, one that weds body and spirit to achieve a greater-than-ever…OK, it sounds stupid when we write it out. As for you, the powerful male urge for independence kicks in as soon as that most vulnerable of moments is over—you either want to bond with the pillow or get the heck out of Dodge. Your brain is wired to exit the emotional relationship once the seed has been planted. So to speak—er, she's on the pill, right? Or a sponge or something. Right? (Now that's worth losing sleep over.)

WHAT'S THE BIG DEAL ABOUT…JOHN CUSACK?

Women have their individual movie-star crushes (Brad Pitt, Richard Gere, David Duchovny), but the one with the broadest appeal is a much more regular Joe: John Cusack. Huh? He's not outrageously good-looking, he doesn't have a body of steel, he's kind of pasty, and he's rarely seen toting a machine gun. But this unlikeliest hunk has the kind of every doofus appeal that's right up many girls' alleys. "Tom Cruise might be better looking, but women sense that he doesn't have the personality to match," suggests John Sellers, author of *PCAT: Preparation for The Pop Culture Aptitude Test.* "John Cusack is the complete package: cute, funny, charming, intelligent. Tom Cruise is fling material; John Cusack is boyfriend material." Can you cash in on Cusack's Casanova cachet? (Can you even say that five times fast?) Yes, you can: Use this chart to steal a few winning moves from Cusack's playbook.

Movie: Better Off Dead
Cusack move: "Cooks" a TV dinner for the fancy French chick and serenades her with his saxophone at a fast-food restaurant.
the lesson: Show off whatever talents you've got in funny, creative ways—it doubles their impact, because it shows you spent some time thinking about her and only her.

Movie: One Crazy Summer
Cusack move: Helps Demi Moore raise enough money to save her grandmother's house.
the lesson: Make her life crises your own. Get her little brother a job or assist her with a work project, and you prove you're interested in her for more than her zipper.

Movie: Say Anything
Cusack move: Stands outside Ione Skye's bedroom window with "their song" blasting on his stereo.
the lesson: Declare your love in embarrassing public ways.

Dating her might just be about the sex, but if you trumpet your affection, it proves you're proud to be with her.

Movie: Midnight in the Garden of Good and Evil
Cusack move: Plays coy with Alison Eastwood to find out what kind of flowers she likes.
the lesson: Engage in complex romantic gestures—they'll be remembered forever. (Remember, your romantic worth is the sum of the anecdotes she can tell her friends about you.)

Movie: Grosse Pointe Blank
Cusack move: Gets Minnie Driver in the sack and proceeds to give her an "airplane ride," balancing her on his feet so she can "fly."
the lesson: Be playful at inappropriate moments—it takes the edge off stressful situations and feels as if you're specifically trying to put her at ease. Girls like that.

Field Her Toughest Questions

"Sometimes I hear questions coming out of my mouth like, 'Does this dress make me look like I'm pregnant?' and I'm not even really looking for an answer," explains (sort of) Geri, 28, an aerobics instructor in Richmond, Virginia. "It's more about me: I'm expressing my mood. I'm probably worried or insecure, so those feelings pop out in weird ways."

Ah, so *that's* why she gets pissed when you reply, "No, you look fine. Now could you *please* get your fat ass in the car?" But what can you do: Faced with impossible questions and a ticking clock, how can you answer without sparking a brush fire? **Answer: Dig deep, find out what she's *really* asking, and get bonus points for extreme Superman-like perception. Here's the road map.**

When she asks: "Do I look fat/short/weird/like Roseanne before plastic surgery?"
She's really saying: Anything from "I'm in a bad mood and I don't want to go wherever we're going tonight" to "I'm not getting enough compliments and reassurance from you, so here's your big chance, big guy." If she rarely asks these types of questions, it's probably situational. "I end up asking those questions when we go out with his buddy Phil and Phil's model-like girlfriend who's still in college," says Tina, 32, a financial manager in Salt Lake City. But this question can also be chronic. Says Jenny, 26, an aspiring actress in Chicago: "My boyfriend is not liberal with the compliments. So I may be feeling like my new blue skirt is sexy, but after he shows up and fails to say anything, I start to wonder if my thighs look weird. I know it's stupid, but I'm fishing for a compliment!" The best response? "I like the guy who just cuts me off—shhh!—like Dr. Evil in *Austin Powers*," says Rachel, 29, a writer in New York City. "It's as though he's saying, 'That question is so ridiculous I'm not even going there.'" But Tina prefers more realism. "He usually says, 'Well, if your legs are bigger, I sure can't see it.' It's a good answer because I'm hyperaware of my body, but maybe no one else can see my five-pound weight changes...I can buy that."

YOUR BRAIN IS WIRED TO EXIT THE EMOTIONAL RELATIONSHIP ONCE THE SEED HAS BEEN PLANTED.

When she asks: "What are you thinking?" or "What does *that* look mean?"
She's really saying: If this question is posed with intensity, she's asking about the relationship, not whether your furrowed brow is due to a dip in the stock market. "I ask him, 'Hey, what's up with you?' when we're hanging out and he's gone all quiet for a while," explains Yolanda, 27, a singer in Brooklyn, New York. "When a guy goes quiet it's unnerving, as though he's about to break bad news to you." Most of the time when she asks this question, she's already decided that she wants to turn the conversation toward your relationship, so responding with, "Nothing," or "I was just getting a little misty remembering Barry Sanders," won't cut it. "My boyfriend has learned to ask the question right back at me, which is fine because then I can say, 'Well, I was thinking about how we never go out just the two of us,' or whatever," says Juliette, 30, a lawyer in Omaha.

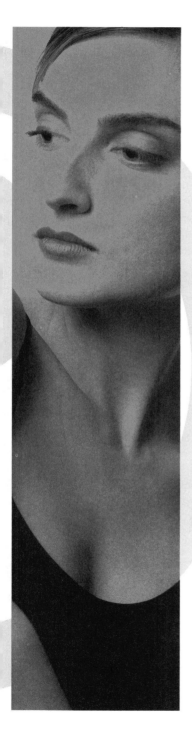

When she asks: "Are you attracted to her?" or "Do you think she's pretty?"

She's really saying: If she's pointing to Cameron Diaz on the big screen, you can relax a little: She's digging for information about your tastes, but she knows the girl's out of your league; there's no danger to her, so you're free to speak your mind. Tactfully. "When he said Cindy Crawford was hot but that in person she probably looked like an amazon freak, man, that was the right answer," confesses Dawn, 21, a student in Indianapolis. "I'm really petite, so he was being consistent and—I hope—honest!"

*But...*if she points to a woman at a party or mentions someone you both know personally, be on your guard. Again, she's seeking information, but comparing herself to a real-world girl is a sign she's feeling insecure, so your praise of the other woman's Scandinavian bone structure could read like a betrayal. On the other hand, pretending a pretty girl is pond scum will just erode your credibility, so don't bullshit her. "I know I stack up in the middle somewhere beauty-wise," explains Rachel. "So while he shouldn't say, 'You're the most gorgeous woman on the planet,' I *do* like to hear, 'She's pretty, but you're the one I like to play hooky with on Friday afternoons.'"

When she asks: "I don't care... what do *you* want to do?"

She's really saying: She may truly not care whether you two rent *The Matrix* or *Shakespeare in Love.* She could be weary and want to get the hell away from the video store's annoying fluorescent lights. Or she may actually have an opinion but is afraid of seeming too demanding. "I like to be low maintenance, so even though I want Mexican food, I'll compromise in my head and rationalize that we'd have to go all the way across town and then we'd miss *Friends,* and Chinese is cheaper anyway, yadda yadda," explains Deirdre, 21, an art student in Savannah. "My last boyfriend finally got me to say what was really on my mind by asking, 'In an *ideal world,* what would you want to do at this point?' It sounds dumb, but then I felt OK throwing my ideas out there because then we could scale down the 'ideal' plan together and I wasn't being a high-maintenance bitch."

HOW TO PLAY HER MOOD SWINGS

As you well know, you only have two moods: good and bad. But women have a whole smorgasbord, not all of them rational by a long shot. Instead of complaining, here's how to play her changing moods to your carnal advantage.

Her mood: Shaken (almost got sideswiped by bread truck)
Your move: Hold her tightly, brush the hair back from her face, and say soothing things like, "It's OK, I'm here." Check for minor injuries.
Why it works: She craves a protector and hero. And here you are: one of those *ER* guys, but in the flesh!
Sex bonus: Heightened adrenaline rush; plus, you come off like Superman even if you perform like Jimmy Olsen.

Her mood: Stressed out (favorite characters on *Ally McBeal* aren't doing what she wants)
Your move: Break out the lotion and give her a foot massage, soothingly working your way up her legs. (Slowly, pardner: Race for the dirty bits and you'll upset the applecart.) Say, "You have such cute little feet," even if they're covered with coarse hair and stink like a bloated dead dog rotting in a sewer pipe.
Why it works: Her last beau wouldn't touch her feet with a 10-foot pole.

The Four Things Women Really Want

You want to be her superhero and do everything humanly possible for her. But, see, that's the *problem*. You're exerting effort trying to *do* things for her, when that's not what she really wants. "Men are led to believe that doing things for women is what counts," says Elyse Goldstein, Ph.D., a psychologist in New York City. But women are more impressed by thought than by deed. It's nice that you can lift the couch single-handedly, but what *really* blows a woman away is when you remember that her parents met in Guadeloupe—which is just the type of effluvia you can't possibly be expected to remember. Here, the intangibles that are a thousand times more appreciated than your ability to install a garbage disposal (not that we don't love that too, you understand):

We want you to tune in. Women thrive on personal interaction and are paranoid about not being heard in the big, bad man's world. That half ear you give a buddy while playing pool won't cut it. She wants both ears and some eye contact for good measure. Be there.

We want you to ask personal questions. We need it...bad. Your girl realizes you don't ask other guys about personal matters, but she lives in a world where it's perfectly appropriate to tell someone she's just met that she hasn't had good sex in six months—it's how women bond. Hint: If you think a topic is too personal (her family, her grooming habits, her dating history), you're probably right on target, so go ahead and ask her!

We want unique compliments. No-brainer praise, like how her great legs make *you* weak in the knees, has its place; but if you're The One, she wants to know that you're noticing things the average catcalling construction worker isn't. Even if her hair only looks microscopically different to you, it's as different as Indy versus stock car to her. Her perfume, the sexy bend of her elbow, her sense of humor are all eminently praiseworthy. You know those moments when your gal does something unexpectedly wild or hilarious or amazing, and you quietly think to yourself, *God, that's so cool that she did that*? Well, say something. You'll score more points than you ever dreamed possible.

We want to be your only babe. Women know you're going to notice other women. (Surprise, surprise: We notice other guys, too.) But when you stare at someone else—and a single extra microsecond is all it takes to qualify, because you're out with her, dammit, and all other women are supposed to be wallpaper—she just can't help thinking you'd rather be with the bimbo. You have a human right and a biological imperative to look at other women, but we're asking you, as part of your commitment to us, to make a constant effort to pretend they're men. Don't let any other girl catch your eye; it symbolizes you're not 100 percent "ours." If you're desperate for a fix, just wait till we're in the rest room, then gawk to your heart's content.

Her Five Primal Fears

Why does your gal sometimes get panicky and paranoid when everything seems to be going well for her? In case you're curious about what's really going on in her head when she sighs wistfully, "It's nothing honey—nothing that you can help with," here are the secret fears she may, believe it or not, honestly and truly *not feel like talking about*. You have been warned.

Fear #1 She'll be a bad mom. The brunt of child rearing is still likely to fall on her, and she may be worried that her skills won't be up to snuff. Even if kids are still a decade away, it comes out in little ways. "I come home from work and then go right back out again to meet friends, and I feel so guilty because I'm totally neglecting my little cat!" says a freaked-out Sunny, 28, a travel agent in Boston. It matters now because nurturing is completely at odds with careering: To be a great mom she'll

Sex bonus: With all that pent-up stress energy, she should be up for a vigorous pelvic workout.

Her mood: Giddy (found righteous footwear bargain)
Your move: As she jabbers on about the details, open your eyes really wide, say, "No way!" and cheer her on/hug her/high-five her as appropriate.
Why it works: Women desperately want to share every emotion with someone, and more important, your lady wants proof that you're as excited as she is. So when she's blissin', second that emotion and you fulfill the role of her best friend. You're in like Flynn.
Sex bonus: Happy vibes mean she'll be aerobically charged and open to that new trick you're dying to try.

Her mood: Fuming (bitchy girl at work looked at her funny again)
Your move: Take her out to dinner, pump her full of wine, and let her rant until she calms down. Be supportive, but don't offer any quick-fix revenge scenarios involving handguns or bear traps—she'll think you're not taking her emotions seriously.
Why it works: She needs to talk it out, because women aren't hep to the quick fix of popping an offender in the jaw.
Sex bonus: No talking... just grunts!

need to be a selfless giver, but to get ahead in her career she needs to be a selfish taker. The closer the two roles converge, the more inner turmoil it's going to cause.

Fear #2 She'll turn into her mom. She loves her mom, but she also knows all her mom's strange tics and is starting to notice them in herself, just the way you've started to make that groaning noise your dad lets loose each time he has to lift himself off the couch. "Lately I've found myself blathering on to strangers about my personal life—like they care!" says Angela, 29, a manager at a travel agency in Rochester, New York. "My mom used to do that and I'd roll my eyes." She may ask you at some point to alert her when she's acting like her mother, but to avoid unnecessarily stoking this flame, don't tell her unless there's immediate personal gain in it for you (e.g., "Honey, remember how your mom never lets your dad go to Vegas with his friends?").

Fear #3 She'll lose her looks. This damn society—OK, magazines like ours—place such a premium on female youth and beauty that it's hard for women to maintain any self-worth after, let's call them, "her *Maxim* years." Now, if you're in love with this girl, once a babe, always a babe—she'll just be older, like you. Still, she's seen this train coming all her life, and the first gray hairs, the first eye-corner wrinkles, and the first irreducible cellulite will freak her out. Don't try to comfort her with the sensible argument about the inevitability of aging: It's no comfort to her, because there's a lot more emotion than logic running through your old lady's—er, your gal's—hot-blooded body.

WHAT'S THE BIG DEAL ABOUT...
VARIOUS CHICK STUFF?

What: Fuzzy slippers
Why: We prefer pampering to practicality.
What: Hair accessories, clips, barrettes
Why: It's the closest we'll ever get to wearing a tiara.
What: Silver tea service
Why: OK, even if we can't have a tiara, we can drink tea like royalty.
What: Talking on the phone
Why: Because we can't rely on you to provide any gossip, now can we?
What: Colored appliances
Why: They remind us of our Easy-Bake Oven.
What: Houseplants
Why: They allow us to exercise

Our desires must sometimes seem strange to you, men of Mars: those paper doilies we put out when guests come over, the taste of tofu, the way we'll tear your arm out of its socket to point out some chair with ducks and daisies painted on it. Even we don't know why we love all that crap...but we gathered the girls and got their best guesses.

nurturing qualities on something that won't talk back and leave dirty socks all over the place.
What: Cookbooks we read but never cook from
Why: We cling pathetically to the idea that we could be Martha Stewart if we really wanted to.
What: A bed overflowing with dozens of pillows
Why: It makes us feel like heroines in a naughty French novel.
What: Bubble baths
Why: They let us lounge in the tub without being confronted by our supposed body flaws.
What: Pretty little boxes
Why: They keep clutter at bay, but stylishly.
What: Your old button-down shirt
Why: It's a token symbol that "he's mine, baby." Bonus:

Fear #4 You'll leave her for a younger woman. Getting older wouldn't be a problem, of course, if nubile young competition for her man's eyes didn't keep cropping up. Even if she feels like she has you wrapped around her little finger most of the time, she knows there's one creature who can snap that string in half—The Younger Woman. "It started in high school when I was a sophomore and all those fresh-faced freshman girls showed up and stole our men," says Kristina, 24, a graphic designer in Providence. She can't compete with a tauter tummy and cheerleader, um, cheeks. Feel free to refer to any gorgeous young chippie you see as "silly" or "stupid," and you might even get a back rub for your troubles.

Fear #5 She'll drop all her goals and settle. Generations of women before her fought and died—well, fought—for her freedom. That's a burden. She's been told she can be anything she wants to be, but is it OK to end up a suburban soccer mom with varicose veins and an IRA? What if she just works part-time at a job she sort of likes, raises a couple kids, and takes way too much pleasure in gardening? Would that be so wrong? She can't decide whether to climb the ladder, ease herself back down, or settle for a comfy rung in the middle...so she's hanging on for dear life. And with women's lack of upper-body strength, it's no wonder she's cranky!

lingering scent of your cologne.

What: Potpourri

Why: We dig flowers so thoroughly that even the dead ones excite us.

What: Padded, satiny hangers

Why: We all watched *Mommie Dearest.*

What: Scented candles

Why: Girls think fire is fun, too—this combines fire with perfume.

What: Men in pajamas

Why: The "dressed" aspect suggests, however hopelessly, that a man might be in bed with us for cuddling and chat, not just sex and sleep.

What: The word *spa*

Why: It connotes absolute pleasure and indulgence (compare with male equivalent, *casino*).

What: Small tins of seashell-shaped soaps

Why: We cling to the old-school notion that the thing that washes you clean should *be* clean, not a grimy sliver of Irish Spring.

What: Monogrammed towels

Why: They make us feel like the queen of the castle, based on all that Virginia Woolf *A Room of One's Own* crappola.

What: Fancy-schmancy stationery

Why: It's a self-esteem boost, because it suggests that we're important enough, rich enough, and armed with enough corresponding friends to warrant owning our own paper.

What: Fancy wine/martini/daiquiri glasses

Why: Because wine is not wine when it's in a mug.

What: Tiny purses that barely hold anything

Why: They emphasize that we have enough power over men to make them hold everything bigger than a credit card for us.

What: Outlet malls/sales

Why: They help us stretch any clothing budget to gain a tiny edge in our lifelong cutthroat competition with gal pals.

What: Manicures

Why: Quality pampering that's cheap and quick.

What: Godiva chocolates

Why: Luscious food, tiny packages, fancy gold paper—it's three of our favorite things, all rolled into one!

What: Crisp, overembroidered "guest towels" too tiny to use

Why: Our moms had 'em.

What: Shoes

Why: They are our baseball cards. Now do you get it?

Why Do Women Talk So Much?

Silence is golden—too bad no one told your gal, huh? Here, Helen Fisher, author of *Anatomy of Love* and *The First Sex*, explains that it's basic biology that makes her blather on. She babbles because...

...She's on estrogen. Fisher says that when a woman's level of this hormone increases, so does her urge to articulate. In other words, prepare yourself for a lot of reassuring nodding around the middle of her monthly cycle.

...She's the mommy. Who taught the cave kids the alphabet when you guys were out spearing wild boars? She did. "Women's ability with words partly comes from millions of years of holding a baby up in front of her face, reprimanding it, cajoling it, and educating it with words," explains Fisher.

...She started sooner. Biological and social influences got her gabbing when she was just a young girl. "Studies show that little girls speak sooner, with more grammatical accuracy, and with more words per utterance," says Fisher.

...She craves intimacy. Yes, women can feel intimate with you just from the sweet silent moments when you walk along holding hands. But women experience more intense intimacy from face-to-face talking. (She'd agree to a threesome in a heartbeat if you meant her, you, and her best girlfriend sitting around a table conversing.)

...She likes the sound of her own voice. Fisher explains: "Because of a woman's tremendous skill with words, she simply gets a charge out of talking. And when others sit and listen, she regards that as intimacy." Oh, brother.

HOW TO GLAZE OVER WITHOUT GETTING BUSTED

You can't pay attention to every single thing she says—tuning in to your chickadee's 24-hour talkfest would mean giving up every other activity in your life. So if you've zoned and she just asked, "Are you listening? What was the last thing I said?" play the odds.

She's probably talking about:

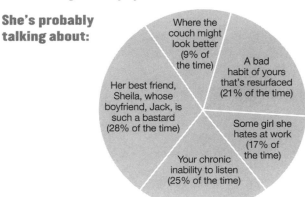

Where the couch might look better (9% of the time)

A bad habit of yours that's resurfaced (21% of the time)

Her best friend, Sheila, whose boyfriend, Jack, is such a bastard (28% of the time)

Some girl she hates at work (17% of the time)

Your chronic inability to listen (25% of the time)

How to Play Her Monthly Cycle

The chocolate binges, the "I'm so fat" confrontation, the whining and general bitch-iness: It's not her fault she's in the throes of hormone swings. But don't just sit there and suffer. Information is power—a knowledge of the inner workings of her hor-mones can help you predict her moods and take advantage accordingly. Hint: If you're not sure when "Aunt Flo" is coming, check her birth control pills (the seven different-colored pills mark her red-letter days), or check her calendar (most women will mark the expected date with a little *P* or a flower).

Days 1–4: Confess a screwup.

With estrogen and progesterone levels at their lowest, your gal's as free of hormon-al influences as she'll ever be. Forgot to feed her fish, God rest its soul? Fess up now.

Days 9–12: Stay out of her way.

A testosterone spike lets her finish 10 projects at work, spend two hours at the gym, and balance the checkbook. Kick back and watch something on the tube; pick up your feet when the vacuum cleaner rolls by.

Days 13–15: Romance her.

When she's ovulating, your gal's in heat, biologically speaking: Her boobs are at their biggest, and her sex drive is high. With estrogen peaking, she'll really be into tender, romantic lovemaking. Ya, stud.

WOMEN THRIVE ON PERSONAL INTERACTION AND ARE PARANOID ABOUT NOT BEING HEARD IN THE BIG, BAD MAN'S WORLD.

Days 21–25: Go for it.

High on testosterone and progesterone, low on estro-gen, a woman's at her most guylike in this stage: She'll enjoy a high-energy romp in the hay—or anywhere else!

Days 26–0: Work late.

Total PMS land, dude: Wear a cup, and keep a low profile. But you knew that.

Man-Handling Her Meltdown

When girls go loony tunes, it's never a pretty sight. You want to run, hide, rend your clothes, and throw dust on your head...but you've got to stay and make it all better because you're a man, not a coward, dammit. And we love you for that. What follow are true tales of emergency amateur psychology from guys who stared their ladies' madness in the face and talked them off the ledge. In other words, a gallery of self-made heroes.

   "It was two years ago, and my wife was yelling at me all day long. It was swel-tering hot in our apartment, and no matter what I did that day, I did it wrong. I gave up trying to do anything or say anything comforting at all, in fact, because I knew she was hot and miserable and pissed at the world for *some* reason. Finally, when she sat down for a minute, I walked over and sat down next to her with my hands behind my back. She looked at me, and I unveiled the ice cube I'd been cupping and held it against the back of her neck. She said, 'Awww,' and melted into my arms."
—John, 25, graduate student, Boston

"She had just gotten off the phone with her lawyer—we were dating, but she was going through a long, nasty divorce—and she burst into tears. I'd never seen my supermellow woman freak out: She pounded her little fists on the table and was screeching through gritted teeth. I kept trying to ask what he'd said and what was wrong, but I finally figured out that she didn't want to share it just then. So I walked over, sat down at her feet, and stroked her knees until she stopped crying. Then I just helped her into bed and held her until she fell asleep." —Steve, 36, trade union organizer, San Francisco

"My girlfriend is, frankly, a drama queen. Now I know what to do, but early on in our relationship, she completely wigged out when I was at her apartment. She had just received an E-mail that someone else was getting a commission that she deserved, and she went ballistic. She threw papers around, brushed all the magnets off the fridge, and knocked over a lamp. I stood there silently, thinking, *OK, what would her sister—who's also her roommate—do?* So I started shouting, too: 'How could they do that to you? That was your account!' Maybe it made her realize how ridiculous she was being, or maybe by yelling I was no longer a good 'audience' for her, but it worked. She talked about it for another 15 minutes, and then we split a pitcher of beer and she was back to just queen, no drama." —Todd, 29, engineer, Little Rock, Arkansas

The Upgrade: No Messy Breakups

Not every relationship can be The One, and sometimes you've got to say goodbye. Understood. All we ask, though, is that you do it right, so we don't have to trash your car, call you like psychos for six months, or blacklist you with all our hottie friends. As Kenny Rogers says, "Know when to hold 'em, when to fold 'em, know when to walk away, know when to run."

Our DOs and DON'Ts for breaking up right:

DO stick to your guns. We can tell when things aren't the same—face it, we probably knew it before you did—so if you've decided you want out, don't leave us hanging in *Why-is-he-acting-like-this?* limbo. Choose an exact date that you're going to dump us and do it, advises Lee Covington, the female author of *How to Dump Your Wife* (Fender Publishing Company, 1996). (Imagine getting caught reading *that* little tome in the john.) Ideally, you want a clean break that leaves her as happy with you as possible so none of the bad things mentioned in the intro will happen. This means being gentle but firm. "And don't keep going back and sleeping with her once you've called it off," adds Covington. (Damn.)

YOU HAVE A HUMAN RIGHT AND A BIOLOGICAL IMPERATIVE TO LOOK AT OTHER WOMEN.

DO tell her in person. Unless you've been dating less than three months, in which case a phone call saves you both the hassle and stress, you've got to execute this one eye to eye. First, this reassures her

that you value her enough as a person to take the time and discomfort to meet with her. Second, if you don't, she'll want to see you one last time, whether it's to cry or scream or just to see you shuffle your feet and squirm uncomfortably. Trying to phone it in just prolongs her pain...and yours.

DO be vague. If you've blindsided her with this news, she'll suddenly start rewinding in her mind, wondering why she didn't see the clues. That's when she'll start asking for details—e.g., "Is it because I dragged you to my cousin's wedding, or because I yell when you're late?" That's a six-hour mine field; do damage control by keeping the talk general—e.g., "I can't really explain it. It's just a feeling I have that something is just missing between us, that we just don't click."

DO keep it brief. She's going to chew on everything you say during the breakup for the next few weeks, so don't blather on and on or she'll interpret the energy you put into the explanation as a sign that you still have feelings for her. Scary, isn't it? Firmer's the way to go. "I could just tell by the finality in his voice and the way he didn't want to launch into a discussion that it was a done deal," says Melinda, 31, an electronic illustrator in Seattle. "The next morning I appreciated it because if we had rehashed it, I would have started crying—his way meant that I didn't wind up blubbering like a fool."

DO tell her she's not The One for you. Remember what Sean Connery and Christopher Lambert said in *Highlander*: "There can be only one." Women, focused on finding The One even if they say they're not, understand this concept. A nice line: "You're so perfect, but you're just not perfect for me." This lets her know the curtain is closing but doesn't undermine her self-worth. A bad one: "I'm just not ready for this kind of commitment." She'll tell you there's no pressure and offer to scale it back, and you'll either have to backpedal, or she'll let you escape and then have your car filled with concrete two months later, when she spots you involved with someone else.

DON'T pull a vanishing act. You can't start ignoring her and pretend "it just sorta slipped away"—this is your decision, so be a man and defend it. "If he'd just said, 'You know, doll, I think you're great, but it's just not working out,' I would have felt rejected, yes, but with the dignity of knowing where I stood," explains Nancy, 27, a freelance writer in Brooklyn, New York.

DON'T lie about the other woman, if there is one. Even if your "overlapping" babe lives in another state, the gal you dumped for her is going to find out eventually—the women's network is more pervasive than the CIA. And then you're in deep doo-doo. "I had finally accepted his excuse that he couldn't commit because he'd just gotten out of a seven-year relationship. But then I find out two months later that he's *living with* his new girlfriend—whom I now realize he'd started hanging out with while *we* were still dating," says Madison, 29, a writer in San Francisco. "After I finished crying, I got mad. Do all of our mutual friends know what he did? You bet they do, because I called everyone to vent!"

DON'T try to cheer her up. "He actually told me, 'Hey, there are a lot of great guys out there,'" says Lauren, 34, a lawyer in Washington, D.C. "It reminded me that, once again, I was going to have to go back to the guy drawing board." Women don't look at breaking up as simply the end of a relationship; they look at it as rejection and failure. Let her be miserable—you can't simultaneously deliver bad news and play Mr. Sunshine.

Similarly, resist the temptation to say anything hopeful like, "Who knows, maybe someday..." or "Maybe if we lived in the same city..." It may hurt her more now to hear that your relationship can't be resuscitated, but she'll respect you more for it later. "Ben said he wanted to break up and I asked him if he loved me, and he paused and said, with a sad voice, 'No,'" says Harriet, 27, a program director in Charlotte, North Carolina. "I respected him for being honest and for emotionally cutting me loose so I could meet someone who does love me—we're still friends, three years later."

DON'T dive into dividing up your stuff. If she has some of your things and you have hers, tough—be cool and she'll be only too happy to dump all your stuff out on the lawn for you. "He dumped me, and then 10 seconds later he actually asked for his REM CDs back! I felt like I'd just been fired and security was about to escort me out the door," says Ricki, 25, a store manager in Madison, Wisconsin. Try to subtly get your stuff back before D-day; then hold out for the rest and hope for the best.

DO keep your distance. Too many nice guys try to remain friends with their ex-gal right after the breakup. You can't break up with her and then ask her to help you shop for a new interview suit. All bets are off after the breakup, at least for many months. "You just dumped me. The last thing I want to hear is that you want to be my damn friend," explains Winnie, 25, a legal assistant in New York City. If a friendship grows later, organically, after all the chemistry and weirdness has died down, then hooray for you. But until that time, stay out of harm's way.

chapter seven

Win Her Over

Getting what you want from the woman you love

Now that you've had a look inside your gal's darling but twisted little noggin—and now that you've stopped your primal screaming—how can you use what you've learned about her weird little world to create a give-and-take environment in your relationship? One in which she doesn't sulk when you run out the door to play poker with the boys, or hurl a pan at your head when you suggest that maybe her tomboyish gal pal might want to come over and play bedtime club sandwich? How can you create a harmonious, shag-filled existence with her in which piddling arguments about the garbage disposal don't escalate into bench-clearing, cop-summoning megabrawls?

In this chapter, we'll help you move beyond simple understanding to real devious manipulation. All the ingredients for whipping up a chick-specific Jedi mind trick are right at your fingertips. You'll learn to disable her defenses, avoid time-wasting communication trouble, and quickly accomplish what you want. (A club sandwich, for example, might be nice...)

Expert Moves
to Keep Her Soothed

You want hassle-free cohabitation; you want to forge a more perfect union. But can you keep her smiling without ending up a whipped, purse-carrying, vacuum-volunteering wonderboy? Of course you can. Just prove you're a sensitive love machine with these expert moves.

1. Call her exactly once every time you go testosterone carousing with the boys. One call establishes that you're thinking about her no matter where you are, without raising her expectations that you're going to check in every time you get a free moment. "I don't want a mama's boy who calls from every bar, but I don't want to feel like his mom worrying if he's forgotten his own number," says Gabby, 27, a brand manager in White Plains, New York.

2. When she starts talking about her feelings, interrupt to ask shrink-like questions. These include: "How did that make you feel?" and "Do you think she could just be projecting her own feelings?"

"If I wanted to talk to a mute, I'd just tell the fish about my day," sighs Alexandra, 31, a playwright in New York City. Your asking questions will ironically shorten your punishment, because it won't take her as long to feel satisfied she's said her piece. On the flip side, if you don't break in with a few questions, she'll gradually start to think you don't care and are just trying to keep the conversation short so you can get back to your damn game.

3. Compliment the not-so-obvious. Instead of looking her over from head to toe and picking a body part to compliment, think of "invisibles" like her sense of humor or her dedication to her work. And instead of complimenting, say, the food she cooks—that's expected; you'd do the same for a male buddy if any of your pals could cook— throw in a mention about the way she arranges that food or sets such a beautiful table. "My ex-boyfriend used to tell me I was the ultimate hostess because I could work a room

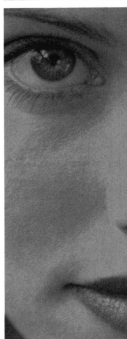

YOU CAN KEEP HER SMILING WITHOUT ENDING UP A WHIPPED, PURSE-CARRYING, VACUUM-VOLUNTEERING WONDERBOY.

without being too obvious," muses Bonnie, 34, a business manager in Los Gatos, California. "I really miss him." Aw.

4. When it's time to apologize, just apologize. Don't stammer half-baked explanations; you're humiliating yourself for nothing. Why? Because excuses —no matter how good—are not what she wants to hear. Unlike guys, women don't welcome logistical explanations about how whatever happened was partly out of your control. The reality is that she thinks that if your apology is not total, it's not heartfelt. "I want to hear him say that he fucked up!" insists Tara, 26, a teacher in Seattle. "Otherwise it's not a real apology." So go on and symbolically abase yourself: "I was stupid. I'm a bad boy. I'm sorry—it won't happen again." Three Hail Marys and you're free as a bird.

5. Clean something in secret. Every so often, give something a good scrub (the bathroom, the fridge, the microwave, etc.). But here's the key: Don't say a word about it. "Opening up the refrigerator to discover that my fiancé had secretly scrubbed the grunge off the bottom shelf is better than anything he could buy me at the mall," says Kimberly, 26, a researcher in Pine Brook, New Jersey. Wanting points for your cleanups implies that housework is her job and you're being a good sport by helping her out. In the same spirit, never, *ever* refer to what you do around the house as "helping"—you'll be in more trouble than if you'd never left the couch.

6. Take care of her car. No matter how independent she is in the rest of her life, a girl still really likes someone to refill her washer fluid and get her oil changed. "My guy works in an office, but the whole macho grease-monkey thing is really sexy," says Krissy, 24, a product manager in Peoria, Illinois. "It's old-fashioned, but when he comes inside from the garage wiping his dirty hands on a rag, I think, *Hey, it's good to have a man around here!*" Plus, this will win you points with her dad...always a good thing.

7. Be a charmer on the phone. Sure, you've got good phone rapport with

THE THREE TIMES
YOU SHOULD *NEVER* COMPLIMENT HER

Just to be nice. You're only sabotaging yourself: *Women catalog your compliments so they can re-create whatever triggered them in the future.* So if her hair reminds you of Jar Jar Binks when it's down, let her hoist it back up before you tell her it looks beautiful, or you'll be making out with Jar Jar for months. But tell her how sexy she looks in strappy tank tops, and she'll be motivated to keep tantalizing you with them all summer long!

When she's pissed at you. Don't trivialize her anger: She'll see right through your pathetic little ploy to sidetrack her/cheer her up. And although it seems like a logical move, telling her, "You look so cute when you're mad!" or otherwise trying to distract her from the madness at hand will result in a lamp to your head. Duck!

When she's throwing up or otherwise illin'. Yes, your instincts are correct: She's feeling ugly and icky. But she'll never buy that there's anything positive about her appearance when she's laid up in bed or blowing chunks, and to suggest otherwise will only brand you a shameless liar. Concentrate on pampering her physically and compliment the blush in her cheeks later, when it's not the result of a viral fever.

her, but if you're not a jolly gentleman when her family and friends call, *she's* the one who gets an earful. When her mother calls, for example, she doesn't want you to immediately hand over the phone—find out how she's doing. "My boyfriend actually greets my girlfriends and asks about their work—they love him!" enthuses Lena, 30, an assistant resort manager in Vail, Colorado. Likewise, when she's on the line with her best friend, don't interrupt to ask where the Tabasco sauce is: Respect the sanctity of the chick gabfest. In fact, if you start to interrupt and cut yourself short with a "Sorry, sorry!" grimace on your face, you'll actually score points for sensitivity.

Compliments **Made Easy**

Most men go to their graves never knowing the awesome power of simple compliments at unexpected times. Sure, you figured out she needs to hear, "Baby, you look amazing," after she's frantically paraded five different outfits through the

DEFENSIVE STRIKES

Women's brains are hard-wired so that they're incapable of forgetting even the tiniest little damn nitpicky thing. A woman can describe in detail exactly how you accidentally mowed over her new blueberry bushes like it happened yesterday, even though it happened, like, *85 years ago*. So long ago that you've honestly forgotten the event altogether...but hey, odds are she's right. The silver lining to this ominous cloud: She also remembers every little wonderful deed you do. So make the most of her Kodak-perfect memory and do something nice. We'll tell you what you can trade it in for.

Good deed: Send *her* ma a Mother's Day card to thank her for raising such a perfect daughter.
Screwup you've earned: Your devotion demonstration earns you three separate incidents of getting caught ogling other women.

Good deed: Showing up with a small present (a bud vase, a tiny lamp for her bedroom, a pair of pastel-colored knit winter gloves) for no reason other than that you adore her.
Screwup you've earned: You've shown you think about her even when she's not around, so you've earned the right to completely forget to call her when you're out with the guys *or* to show up really, really late for a date.

Good deed: Dancing with her for a few hours in a public place.
Screwup you've earned: You've essentially said in front of the whole world that you love her body, so you've earned the right, one time, to fall into a sex coma 60 seconds after the main event.

Good deed: Helping her set up her homely cousin with one of your buddies.
Screwup you've earned: This deed says that you're aware of the larger world of relationships she's ensconced in, so you've earned two incidents of forgetting to pass along killer gossip.

Good deed: Staining and sealing her entire deck.
Screwup you've earned: After establishing that you are the man of her house, you can now indulge in one incident of arriving at her place drunk from a strip club and yakking all over the bathroom.

living room en route to her high school pal's big wedding. But it's the compliments you slip in on the sly that score the biggest points. And that's important, because the more loved and attractive we women feel, the more we feel like—yep—having sex. Girls gush about their favorite compliments...here's your chance to steal a great idea or two.

"Usually a guy compliments your apartment when he first sees it, but it was so nice that my boyfriend, three weeks after we'd started dating, looked around after we'd made love on my couch and said, 'I really like the way you've arranged your living room; it's really cozy.' Since there was apparently nothing that'd prompted it, it sounded extra sincere." —Chloe, 33, art gallery worker, New York City

"I had finally agreed to go white-water rafting with this guy, and I was so scared I was screaming practically the whole time. But at one point he looked over and yelled, 'You're the best! You're amazing.' I mean, I knew he was going to thank me for agreeing to go, but the fact that he chose a moment when we were in the throes of this crazy adventure to say it made me love him more!" —Anita, 25, fund-raiser for a nonprofit agency, Providence

"My husband was talking with a group of friends at a wedding, and when I walked over and asked what they were talking about, he said, 'I was just pointing out to the guys what a total babe my wife is.' I gave him crap about using the word *babe*, because it's kind of offensive, but secretly I felt so good that Mr. Tough Guy would give me a sweet compliment like that in front of his former fraternity brothers." —Beatrice, 22, day-care associate, Sacramento, California

"My boyfriend is great because he tells me how attractive I am all the time. But that's why it meant so much the other night when I finished describing this complex project I was working on to a group of friends. In the car on the way home he said, 'I love the way your brain works—you explain things like that so well.' I felt like the beauty *and* the brains. It was such a subtle thing for him to pick up on." —Tammy, 33, engineer, Los Angeles

"A lot of guys will give you compliments before and after sex, but my ex-boyfriend used to stop moving inside of me for a second and look in my eyes and say, 'You're so amazing.' Other guys zone out on the physical pleasure so much that you think they've forgotten you're there, so his words right then were much appreciated!" —Karla, 28, editor, Tampa

Goodwill Investment

For those times when you need a big favor from your gal—like calling her to bail your drunk ass out of jail, or asking if your divorcing buddy can crash on the sofa— she might make you pay dearly, depending on how contrite you sound and how big an imposition the favor entails. But lay down some bargaining chips now, and you'll be able to secure big favors later at a much cheaper rate.

The basic plan, to keep it simple: You make a sincere effort to become her number-one fan. Few men can really pull this off, but it's damn romantic, and women will worship you—and let Louie stay as long as he likes—if you can manage it. Good luck...we're all counting on you.

Tip #1: Keep track of her stats.

Pretend it's fantasy-league baseball: Know where she is on the totem pole at work, how her relationship with her sister is going, and what's up with her best friend's so-called marriage. That way, when she gets off the phone with her sis in defeat, you can point out that she shouldn't feel so bad, since she won last week's match. "My boyfriend knows my friend and I are really competitive, so when I point out that she has yet another article in a major magazine, he realizes it's a big deal to me," says Rebecca, 28, a writer in Minneapolis. "That makes me feel like my world's important to him."

FORGIVENESS FILMS –WHY GUYS WERE

Movie: *An Officer and a Gentleman*
Guy crime: Walked out on his blue-collar girlfriend after a big fight.
Movie-guy move: Marched into the factory where she worked and carried her off, to the cheers of dozens of coworkers.
Why it worked: He publicly demonstrated that she was his chosen one while retaining his manly mystique.

Movie: *Jerry Maguire*
Guy crime: Told the girl he loved her, then married her, then blew her off.
Movie-guy move: Brought himself to utter the schmaltziest line of all time, "You complete me," in a room full of whiny divorced women.

Why it worked: He admitted that man cannot live alone, that he needed her—a big female fantasy.

Movie: *The Graduate*
Guy crime: Slept with his girlfriend's mother.
Movie-guy move: Rescued her from a loveless marriage by crashing her wedding.
Why it worked: Reinforced that whole knight-in-shining-armor-rescuing-the-distressed-maiden fantasy.

Movie: *Pretty Woman*
Guy crime: Insulted her with an offer of a full-time position as his kept woman/call girl.
Movie-guy move: Rode up in a shiny limo,

> It's all so easy in the movies: Guy screws up, guy pulls self-effacing but still macho move, guy gets to ride off into her sunset. Why shouldn't your life be the same? Steal a scene from the cinema and get back in her good graces.

Tip #2: Cheer her on.

You've noticed that women get psyched up for big events — they get dressed and re-dressed, they start calling one another to blab about unfolding details — so the next job interview or party she's hosting, get in there with a big foam #1 hand. "My boyfriend woke me up by playing the theme from *Rocky* the morning of an interview I had, and it showed he really understood me. We still joke that I owe him for getting me the job," says Phoebe, 26, a software designer in Seattle.

Tip #3: Sit tight during her postgame show.

Women love to rehash the details of an event, and it's your job, as her fan club, to cheer or bitch right along with her. If she threw her girlfriend a bridal shower, sit with her on the couch as she spills her little guts about the goofy games they played and who brought what present. Don't panic: She'll get bored of retelling the story, too, and eventually let you off the hook, we promise. But no checking your watch.

Tip #4: Be her personal booster.

When her pals and parents ask how her grad-school midterms went, brag about your little team player, who's probably too modest to give herself real props. "After I nailed this big presentation, my boyfriend started calling me 'knock-'em-dead Nicky' and told all our friends at dinner how smoothly it had gone!" says Nicky, 26, a publicist in Greenwich, Connecticut. She'll love that you're willing to witness it all in super slo-mo again. You made the right call!

GRANTED REDEMPTION IN MOVIES

climbed her fire escape, and carried her away.

Why it worked: He managed to be chivalrous but do it her way, too.

Movie: *Romancing the Stone*

Guy crime: Went after the jewel and left the girl to fend for herself.

Movie-guy move: Drove up the street on a sailboat to get her back.

Why it worked: He remembered what she said her dream was and made it come true.

Movie: *Notorious*

Guy crime: Didn't stop her from marrying a Nazi in South America to help the CIA.

Movie-guy move: Rescued her when her husband poisoned her.

Why it worked: He never gave up on her, proving that true love can overcome any obstacle.

Movie: *Splash*

Guy crime: Deserted her after finding out she was a mermaid.

Movie-guy move: Left his human life behind forever to live underwater with her.

Why it worked: Showed he was willing to sacrifice even the air he breathed to be with her.

Movie: *Grease*

Guy crime: Acted aloof around the girl to impress his friends.

Movie-guy move: Earned a letter and dressed up like a jock to try to be the guy he thought she wanted.

Why it worked: Proved he was willing to change for her—that she was more important to him than his image, his reputation, or his friends.

You Screwed Up. Now What?

You've just bungled your way into the doghouse. And you can tell from that sinking feeling in your gut that you're going to need more than a standard apology to make things right with your woman. This blunder is going to require a strategic sorry: zeroing in on exactly which button you pushed, and then—like Superman flying backward around the earth so fast he reverses the events of the previous day— undoing the wrong. We're not talking smoothing things over. We're talking making her forget it ever happened. Fortunately, so many guys screw up on a regular basis that we were able to poll quite a few about their most common transgressions, talk to a bunch of women who have forgiven their men, and bring you the insights of our research in just a few painless pages. Read them and your next domestic squabble will be more of a Grenada than a Vietnam.

Strategies for absolution so total, your woman won't just forgive—she'll forget.

THE MORE LOVED AND ATTRACTIVE WE WOMEN FEEL, THE MORE WE FEEL LIKE— YEP—HAVING SEX.

Screwup #1: She found out you had more sexual encounters in your past than you said.
Her problem with you right now: She fears she doesn't really know you...and she's imagining all the other stuff you must be hiding. Not only that, but you lied to her!
How to press reset: Tell her you were afraid your checkered past would scare her, so you stayed mum. Now, however, she knows the worst, and you're actually relieved, because your relationship can reach "a new level of intimacy." This worked for Matt, 35, a graphic designer in New York City. The only downside, he says, is that she may want to open up about her own wild period, and then you're faced with the equivalent of watching her audition amateur-porn costars. But hey, you'll have been absolved.

Screwup #2: You talked down to her.
Her problem with you right now: She thinks you believe you're a genius and she's a pea brain.
How to press reset: Apologize for the condescending tone of voice—there's never any excuse for that—but then show her why you feel proprietary about the area of expertise in question. First, though, concede her superiority at some other chore (don't make it a grubby task like housecleaning or diaper changing; go for high-end flattery). For example, say, "I surrender control of the banking to you, because if I were in charge of the books, we'd probably have had our doors kicked down by the IRS by now. But when it comes to investing, I've been doing it well for five years, and I think you should give me credit for knowing what I'm doing." (A little guilt never hurts in this situation.)

Screwup #3: You said you'd call, but...

Her problem with you right now: She sat by the phone for 48 hours and assumes you didn't think of her once. This has created a serious power imbalance: She thinks she's 48 times more into the relationship than you are.

How to press reset: "Acknowledge that you blew it, and give a legitimate excuse if you've got one," says John Bridges, author of *How to Be a Gentleman* (Rutledge Hill Press, 1998). But keep it short and sweet. "I was in endless mind-fucking meetings, and I didn't want to call until I could decompress a bit" is better than a litany of lame little problems, all of which got priority over her. Next, restore the balance by clearing the weekend and making specific plans for two. Talk is cheap, but a confirmed hotel reservation puts your money where your mouth is.

Screwup #4: You came too soon.

Her problem with you right now: She thinks you don't care that she ain't gettin' no satisfaction.

How to press reset: "Say, 'I like you so much, I got overly excited,'" says relationship expert Nita Tucker, author of *How Not to Screw It Up* (Three Rivers, 1999). She thinks this is adorable. Then take care of her needs—you know how. Promise that next time you'll make her come twice before you even penetrate. She'll probably settle for once.

Screwup #5: You were late for dinner with her parents.

Her problem with you right now: Everything is all about you. Your life is so important, you've just dissed her *and* the people who gave her life.

How to press reset: A mumbled "sorry" as you take a seat won't work here—you must do serious penance, says Denver psychotherapist Carolyn N. Bushong, author of *The Seven Dumbest Relationship Mistakes Smart People Make* (Villard, 1997). Say, "I'm really sorry that I'm late, and to make up for it, I'd love to take care of the meal—and smile as her dad orders lobster. Next time, phone ahead to the restaurant to tell your party you're running late. It'll save you a couple hundred bucks.

Screwup #6: You talked to a highly doable friend of your girlfriend at a dinner party.

Her problem with you right now: She thinks you want to screw her friend.

How to press reset: She's on to you, pal. We don't normally advocate this sort of thing, but it's time to lie. Tell your girlfriend that Ms. Dream Girl was asking you dumb questions about the stock market, then explain away the mesmerized look you had on your face by saying that your attention was riveted by the ugly black hairs on her upper lip, or her disgusting breath, or the fact that her legs are as big as sequoias—stuff she knows you hate, so it'll have a ring of truth to it. "Then," says etiquette expert Bridges, "say something reassuring like, 'You know you're the only woman for me.'" And try not to say it in a sad way.

Screwup #7: You came to an event seriously underdressed.

Her problem with you right now: She thinks you're a child, you don't take anything seriously, and you don't care enough about how she feels to look good for her.

How to press reset: Remind her that in other areas of your life, you're as adult as her dad is. Then throw yourself on the mercy of her superior sartorial sense. Try: "Look, I work 70 hours a week overseeing $2 million worth of blah-blah-blah, but I'm the first to admit I don't have a clue whether a 'semiformal' calls for pin-

stripes or a party hat." Then tell her that it took you two dress rehearsals to come up with the mess you're wearing (so she knows you made an effort). And cap it with a suggestion that she take you shopping for some impressive duds. Shopping together? You just scored major points.

Screwup #8: You gave her the wrong birthday gift.

Her problem with you right now: She thinks you don't know her at all and that you haven't bothered to try.

How to press reset: Women invest months of time and thought, not cash, on The Perfect Gift for you. So thinking, for example, *Next time I'll go for the whole mink coat instead of just the cuffs and collar* won't help a whit if she's a member of PETA. When she takes you window-shopping around the time of her birthday, this is not a coincidence. She is dropping hide-saving hints. Take notes and poke around: Ask her girl pals and family what she wants. As for the disaster at hand, say, "I can tell you're disappointed and I feel awful, so tell me what you would have liked," suggests psychologist Dory Hollander, Ph.D., author of *101 Lies Men Tell Women* (Harper Collins, 1997). "Then, a couple weeks later, surprise her with it."

FORGET FIGHTING FOREVER

HOW TO NEGOTIATE LIKE A PRO

There are ways to ward off ugly bickering before it bites you both in the ass. We went to two lawyers—Stacy D. Phillips, a divorce attorney in Century City, California, and Stephen M. Greenberg, a divorce attorney in New York City—to bring you their top negotiating tips to keep the peace around your place (and avoid costly legal bills).

Lawyer trick: Show the other party that you understand her desires.

How to use it: When she starts to get pissy, say to her, "I hear what you're saying" and "Let me repeat what you've said so I'm sure I understand" or "It seems to me that you're saying X and Y."

Lawyer trick: Listen more than you speak.

How to use it: Let her talk for a while, and she just might offer a solution or compromise you can happily deal with.

Lawyer trick: If possible, avoid having outside parties negotiate for you—the primary players should try to work it out themselves.

How to use it: Don't involve your friends or let her involve her mother or anyone else in the negotiations. If she starts to draw others in by saying, "Well, Judy says such and such," tell her, "This is important and it's something we need to work out, just the two of us."

Lawyer trick: If things aren't going well during negotiations, offer an alternative settlement—with a cherry on top.

How to use it: There's no way you're going to miss a playoff game to have lunch with her and her mother, so offer to reschedule—and add an afternoon of antique hunting (they hunt; you carry the stuff) to the deal.

Lawyer trick: Avoid cross-examining your opponent. You need to give people an opportunity to back off gracefully and to save face because you can't reach an amicable settlement if your opponent has just been backed into a corner.

How to use it: Don't try to force her to agree with your opinion. Fights between lovers aren't about winning or losing; they're about getting along better in the future. A win might cost you something more important (like sex for a month).

Lawyer trick: If the two parties are stuck, take a break and have each send the other a summary of their arguments.

How to use it: If you're both still pissed about last night's brawl the next morning, when you get to work, shoot her an E-mail briefly explaining that you adore her so much that you get lost or muddled in the emotion when you argue face-to-face. You're taking this chance to write out your feelings so you can express them better, and you hope that she'll do the same because you want to understand her position.

Super Bonus Lawyer trick: Read over the final agreement and congratulate yourselves on having reached a settlement.

How to use it: This helps to prevent other misunderstandings and have true closure on your disagreement. Point out that your relationship has grown as a result of your resolving a conflict *together,* and go over what was decided to make sure that you're both clear on what's expected of you. Then look her in the eye and say, "I'm glad we got this all out in the open—I really feel closer because of it." Congrats: She now loves you even more than Dylan McDermott, the star of *The Practice.*

Screwup #9: In the heat of passion, you tried to, um, enter the back door uninvited.

Her problem with you right now: She's worried that you're bored with your sex life and that you see her as nothing more than an inflatable sex doll.

How to press reset: Never try to make her believe you didn't know where your penis was...do you really want her thinking that? Remedy the situation during or after the act. "You'll have seemed a cad, so switch to cuddling lovemaking, including looking her in the eye," says Bushong. Later, tell her you thought you were so close, she might have wanted to try it (but admit you shoulda asked first).

Screwup #10: You said you'd be home around midnight; you showed up trashed at 4 a.m.

Her problem with you right now: You knew it would piss her off and worry her, and you did it anyway.

How to press reset: It's best to be honest and tell her that, as the shrinks say, you were "acting out." Get her to understand that every once in a while, you need to not be responsible to *anyone* (so she doesn't think you are focusing on her) for a solid eight hours. Don't give her a feeble list of stuff that kept you from the phone. "Take your knocks and deal with it in the morning," Bridges strongly advises. "And then just say you're sorry and you won't do it again, because you know you worried her."

Screwup #11: You weren't supposed to tell anyone about your office romance, but you did.

Her problem with you right now: She feels like she's just a notch on your bedpost.

How to press reset: You've just bragged like a seventh-grade boy...time to act mature, real fast. Offer to take any heat from the suits at work if the word travels up that far. Assure her that you'll tell them it's not just a fling and that if there are to be any repercussions, they should come down on you. The brass will probably not find out, so you'll seem chivalrous without ever having to take a hit for your lady. And if you feel moved to do so, you could also add, "I love you so much I couldn't keep it a secret," which worked for Dave, 26, a lawyer in Brooklyn, New York. Of course, you may want to make sure you're actually in love first...or you'll be stuck with her spending some long nights on top of that copier for many months more than you meant to.

Screwup Insurance

More relationships end around anniversaries than at any other time—usually because you forget and she makes a big deal about it, says Shari A. Betterman, Ph.D., a marriage and family therapist in Beverly Hills, California. "To a woman, anniversaries and gifts are symbols or markers of a dream," she explains. "So if you forget your anniversary, it says, 'I don't love you' and 'I don't care enough about this relationship to remember very personal and important things.'" To keep your honey hanging around, make sure you have a couple of these guaranteed ass-savers socked away where she won't stumble onto 'em. You can thank us later.

FIGHTS BETWEEN LOVERS AREN'T ABOUT WINNING OR LOSING; THEY'RE ABOUT GETTING ALONG BETTER IN THE FUTURE.

Blank cards: Buy a half-dozen different, pretty-on-the-outside, blank-on-the-inside cards in case you forget an important date (like your six-month anniversary) or in case she's stuck in a funk (secretly slip one in her workbag in the morning; reap the rewards that night!).

An item of lingerie, wrapped up:
This will cover you in case you forget a present-buying holiday or just to smooth things over after a big fight. You can always say, "I was going to surprise you with this little satiny number on your birthday next month..." which will get you points for looking like the kind of guy who plans ahead.

A card or trinket *she* gave *you*:
Saving something that she probably thinks you threw away can help prove your love in the middle of an argument. That way you'll have *evidence*. "Honey, if I didn't love you, would I have saved the Pictionary scrap paper that you successfully drew the word *ricochet* on from our second date?"

The double wedding ring: Men lose wedding rings, usually from playing rough

sports or slipping their rings off to lift at the gym. Nope: She won't believe this either, and if you show up naked-knuckled she'll forever assume that gold band is sitting on some floozy's nightstand. Ward off a someday disaster by getting a jeweler to make you an extra—guys have been known to preemptively commission and pick up two wedding rings at the original point of purchase (which works because picking up the rings is a groom task). Just make sure to alternate them for the first year or so, so they wear evenly.

Her vital stats in your wallet: This is the best trick yet devised for foolproofing your gift giving; when it's time to buy her a present, you have all the answers the retailers need to know. Write down her clothing sizes, her ring size, her birth date, your anniversary, her astrological sign, her bra size, her shoe size, her favorite types of flowers, and (if you don't live together) the colors of her bedroom and living room.

How to Tell
What You're Really Fighting About
If you've ever stood there while she screeched and hollered and burst blood vessels, and wondered, *Why the hell does she care this much about where I leave my underwear?* you've guessed that men and women fight differently. Whatever your little tiff is, it's guaranteed to be the tip of an iceberg, because women are usually arguing about emotions, not just events. "Men view an argument through the lens of the issue, but women view an argument through the lens of the relationship," explains Cathleen Gray, Ph.D., a couples therapist and a professor at the Catholic University of America in Washington, D.C. Ah, but which iceberg? Here's how to get to the bottom of what's really bugging her before you sink like the *Titanic*.

FIGHTING DOS AND DON'TS

"There's a reason women don't do as well in court as men do: The legal system is set up for gladiator battle, the way men like to fight," says therapist Cathleen Gray. "But men need to realize that sometimes it's a choice between being right and being happy." So that you don't end up with a curling-iron-shaped dent in your head, these fighting dos and don'ts will help you play gladiator...and play it safe, too.

DO admit, delicately, what's on your mind. If she can tell there's something eating at you, no self-respecting woman will stop until she gets to the bottom of it, so why make her pester you until she's really pissed? "The worst thing my boyfriend does is to keep saying he doesn't want to talk about it and shut me out," says Patricia, 31, a graduate student in Madison, Wisconsin. "Then I have to coax him into talking to me by saying, 'What's wrong, what's wrong?' over and over again until he cracks."

DON'T use intimidation tactics. Threats and bravado may work with the guys, but threaten her and you'll come off like a big bully. If you're getting into that mean mode, get things back on track by forcing yourself to start the next couple of sentences with, "I feel" or "I'm confused because" which are endearingly humble phrases she'll warm up to.

DO listen instead of formulating your comeback. If you're just thinking about the next dig you can get in, you're going to miss out on what she's saying and feeling, and miss a chance to find some common ground.

DON'T look at your watch. It sounds simple, but guys always expect fights to be like fistfights: quick and practical and dirty. But verbal sparring with women is always long and drawn out, because it's a discussion of feelings and emotions. If you're the type that glances at your watch compul-

sively, then just take it off. Once she sees you glancing at it, she'll have a whole other reason to be mad.

DO confess a fault before you accuse her of one. Simply saying, "I know I forget to pay the credit card bill when you don't remind me" before you point out that *she* has bounced two checks this month will soften the blow and make you seem like a loving partner instead of the hated enemy.

DON'T trivialize her sweet, petty little concerns. Yes, it's stupid that she thought you were implying that she was fat when you mentioned how much she loves mashed potatoes, but telling her that her fears are stupid is the quickest way to take her from upset to mad. No matter what's eating at her, once she says it, acknowledge it and reassure her.

DO touch her. She may swat you away if she's really upset, so get in there early. "My fiancé is great because he sits us down on the couch and holds my hands," says Kimberly, 26, a researcher in Pine Brook, New Jersey. "It's hard to say mean and angry things to each other when you're touching in that position."

DON'T say "never" and "always" in a fight. Extreme language like this just fans her flames, so try to stick to the issue at hand (even if she does *always* complain that you *never* do laundry).

DO know when to retreat. If she bursts into tears or if she caught

you red-handed admitting that you *did* have sex with her college roommate three years ago and never told her, give in. You can't win, and if you keep yelling at her while she's crying, you'll be shunned by all people female forever.

DON'T make competitive comparisons. Don't bring up your ex-girlfriends or how she treated her ex-boyfriends. Bringing other people into the fight makes you look pathetic and unable to focus on the real issue at hand.

DO steer clear of name-calling. The names you call her will reverberate in her sensitive head forever, and you'll never be able to take them back. Plus, if she calls you a dick and you show restraint in this area, she'll just feel that much more guilty afterward.

DON'T leave without an understanding. Since you're not fighting to win, but to achieve a deeper understanding of each other, you need to agree and reach a conclusion. If you just let the fight dissipate, it'll only rear its ugly head again. And what a nightmare that would be!

DO follow up. To really put closure on the fight, you have to symbolically acknowledge your understanding of the changed state of your relationship. Do this with a small gift the next day or a simple follow-up phone call, 24 to 48 hours later, to let her know you're still thinking about the fight and what you've learned.

Her gripe: You didn't call when you said you would.
What's really bugging her: You're not making her feel needed. Tell her how important she is to you, but claim you need to be free to be spontaneous sometimes, too. Promise that next time you're tied up on a big office project you'll call her—in fact, you realize now that you could have used her moral support during last week's craziness.

Her gripe: You're a slob.
What's really bugging her: You're taking her for granted. Yes, she hates the way your socks look in the middle of the living room floor, but what those gym socks really do is taunt her into thinking that she's just a live-in maid and sex service. Along with promising to be better in the future, you need to emphasize that you love living with her. Try: "We have such a beautiful home; I know I'm a bonehead for messing it up."

Her gripe: You're always late.
What's really bugging her: She's low on your priority list. If you were at work late or had to finish talking to a friend on the phone, she immediately assumes whatever was keeping you is more important than her. Let her know she's number one in other ways (step out of a big meeting just to call her, for example) and try to clean up your act.

Her gripe: You forgot to make reservations.
What's really bugging her: You're not being the man. Women admit it's a little archaic, but they love it when you take the planning burden off their shoulders completely and choose an event or restaurant, get tickets or reservations, then give them the princess treatment. Screw it up and she feels deposed. Next time, check the reservations, and have a backup in place.

> GUYS ALWAYS EXPECT FIGHTS TO BE LIKE FIST-FIGHTS: QUICK AND DIRTY. BUT VERBAL SPARRING WITH WOMEN IS ALWAYS LONG AND DRAWN OUT.

Get Her to Sexperiment

Maybe you and your woman have been using the missionary position so long you're convinced you could convert a synagogue. But how can you introduce your mate to the thrill of sexploration when she seems perfectly happy with the well-traveled terrain of your ho-hum love life? Well, some ideas are easier than others to plant in her head (not to mention other places). Here, in increasing order of difficulty, are your keys to the kinkdom.

1. Talk her into talking dirty. To get your usually chatty gal to start in on the saucy talk, emphasize that you want her to express herself or tell you what she likes. "As we were taking off each other's clothes, he'd say things like, 'I love kissing your tits,' but he never used any degrading words like *bitch*. Suddenly he whispered in my ear, 'Talk to me, tell me how you feel,'" says Ashley, 25, an actress

in Los Angeles. "I was nervous that I'd sound silly, but after dating so many guys who just wanted a quick screw or didn't listen to me, here was a guy who was urging me to express myself. I tentatively chimed in with, 'I love it when you run your hands across my ass like that,' and now I'm learning to like it more and more."

Danielle, 21, a researcher in Boston, got into it a different way. "I was in a long-distance relationship, so we would send each other these increasingly racy E-mails, and one time when I was visiting him, he'd printed out an explicit one that I'd written," she recounts. "He told me how he kept rereading it because it turned him on, and then he asked if I'd read it to him. As I read it, he slowly took my clothes off. I was turning red reading it because I'd written something like, 'I want to feel your cock inside me and push you into me harder and harder.' It turned him into an animal, and now I volunteer a few phrases when we're in bed because I realize he just loves it." Hint: If she seems really hesitant, make sure she's over 17 and then reassure her that you don't mean for her to say anything pornographic (OK, at least not *yet*); you just want her to tell you how she feels.

2. Get her to get messy. A lot of women prefer having sex showered and shaved and with clean sheets on the bed. But they also love to do things that turn you on, so there is hope of getting down and dirty with your little dish. "My husband of four years surprised me with a weekend trip. He'd mentioned that he wanted to liven up our sex life, but I was feeling really unattractive because I'd gained a little weight," explains Marianne, 34, a chef in Denver. "When we got to our hotel room, he unwrapped this crazy lingerie outfit with garters. He assured me he liked my body better now, because my breasts were fuller and sexier, and he kept having fantasies at work about me in a red bra and him ejaculating on my chest, something we'd never done before. It was a turn-on hearing him verbalize what he wanted. The way he asked—sweetly, softly, earnestly—and the fact that he'd gone to so much trouble so that we could get away from the daily grind clinched the deal. I was a sticky mess at the end (we used lotion when the friction started to hurt my chest), but I must admit that afterward we felt closer." Hint: Let her know during the act how great it is for you. In cases like this she may not be getting any direct physical pleasure, so she needs to be reassured that she's giving you pleasure.

3. Sell her on sixty-nine. Maybe she loves oral sex, giving and receiving, but the simultaneous-deed positioning turns some women off. So how do you woo her into the numbers racket? "When you do sixty-nine, the guy's face—his eyes, his nose—are right there," points out Anne, 26, a creative consultant in Omaha. "My boyfriend kept saying how much he wanted to do it and asked why I didn't. I told him why the vulnerable position made me uptight and said the only way I would try it is if we'd just taken a bath. He said, 'Well, let's just take a bath together,' and we did, right then. Back in bed we were lying on our sides, and I put him in my mouth and he moved my legs apart and suddenly we were doing it, and I've happily been in that position many, many times since."

Meghan, 19, a student in Albany, New York, says she agreed to do it, but only if all the lights were off. "Now I don't mind if the lights are on, but I felt less self-conscious the first time around to be wrapped in darkness." So what have we learned? Ease her into it by letting her set some guidelines; she'll probably ease up on those restrictions over time.

4. Bond with bondage. First, try to avoid the word *bondage*, which has scary connotations. "My boyfriend asked me to do it after two months, and I was horrified because all I could picture were handcuffs ripping into my flesh or him dying with me still attached to the bedpost," explains Carly, 26, an interior decorator in Richmond. She ended up letting her boyfriend tie her up with a silk scarf after he admitted that by not wanting to try new things he felt like she was clinging to her ex's memory. "I was touched by that admission."

He eased her into it by just placing the scarf near the bed, no pressure, and then he tied her wrists together and made love to her very, very slowly. "It was a relief that he made love to me really slowly and kept talking to me, because although the taboo feeling was exciting, I felt vulnerable," she says.

Madeleine, 23, a waitress in St. Louis, says she told her boyfriend he could handcuff her wrists and tie her legs to the bedposts but that she just wanted to have foreplay that way, not sex. "But I found it was really a turn-on because when you're tied up it's all about him touching you and you just get to lie there and moan, so I told him to just leave me tied up for the main event, too," says Madeleine. Hint: Keep asking her if it's OK and if she wants to stop—it'll help reassure her that she's ultimately in control.

> **WOMEN ALSO LOVE TO DO THINGS THAT TURN YOU ON, SO THERE IS HOPE OF GETTING DOWN AND DIRTY.**

5. Turn her on to toys. You may assume that every woman has a vibrator awaiting her in her top drawer. But for a lot of women, you'll be the first one to give them a big buzz, so take it slow. "My boyfriend and I had joked about vibrators, but when he got me one, it seemed so unnatural—it was blue!" exclaims Joanne, 24, a nurse in Cleveland. "He said he thought I'd like it because I like being touched fast and rhythmically, and that he sometimes feels like a failure because it takes me a lot longer to climax than it takes him."

Joanne's boyfriend showed up the next week with an off-white model. "The fact that he'd gone back to the sex shop to get one I'd like better made me realize he cared about making me happy," she says. He eased her into using it by moving the vibrator across her breasts and thighs and then on to more pressing pastures. "It was amazing. I orgasmed a lot faster, too. These days it's usually me who gets it out of the drawer!" Hint: Be prepared for her to turn down your request the first time, but don't give up hope. She may just need a chance to mull it over, so be patient and then gently bring it up again.

6. Knock at the back door. Getting a girl to go anal ain't easy. Most women say it's painful, so be prepared for some prep work. Heidi, 26, a musician in Seattle, went through a major experimental phase with a guy she lived with. Why was she a willing participant in his adventurous antics? "Because he always gave me what most women really want: oral sex. He'd go down on me for an hour, literally, and made me climax two or three times until I felt sort of stoned in love," explains Heidi. She says he brought the topic up casually by saying "he wanted to be inside every part of me, and I knew he meant, uh, back there. One night after he'd gone down on me, we were in the shower, and he slowly turned me around, rubbed the wetness from my front to my behind, and put it in. It was really emotional—I almost cried—and it felt like everything below my stomach was floating. He kept whispering my name and made it clear how amazing it was for him. I was in pain afterward, but he made me a cup of tea and gave me the whole princess treatment."

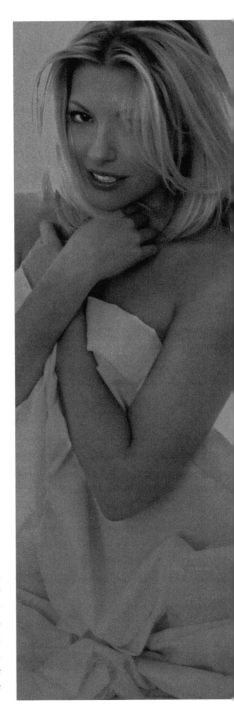

Note: This is a ground not all women want to visit, and if she does do it, she'll probably consider it a gift. "I gave it to him as a birthday present," explains Gini, 27, a medical assistant in Harrisburg, Pennsylvania. "I didn't really want to, but he'd mentioned it many times, so I could tell it would make him crazy with joy. We took precautions like using lubrication, but he's a big guy and partway into it—or into me, rather—I had to tell him to stop because the pain, the stretching and almost ripping feeling, was too awful." But even though it didn't come to fruition, Gini's boyfriend still expressed his appreciation. "He was thrilled that I'd been willing to try it, and I have to admit it created a weird little bond because it was something I'd never tried with anyone else."

Hint: Make sure you've established that if she starts to feel uncomfortable, you'll stop immediately; then stick to the rules. If she says, "Wait, I'm not ready," jump back and then wait until she says "go" to jump back in again.

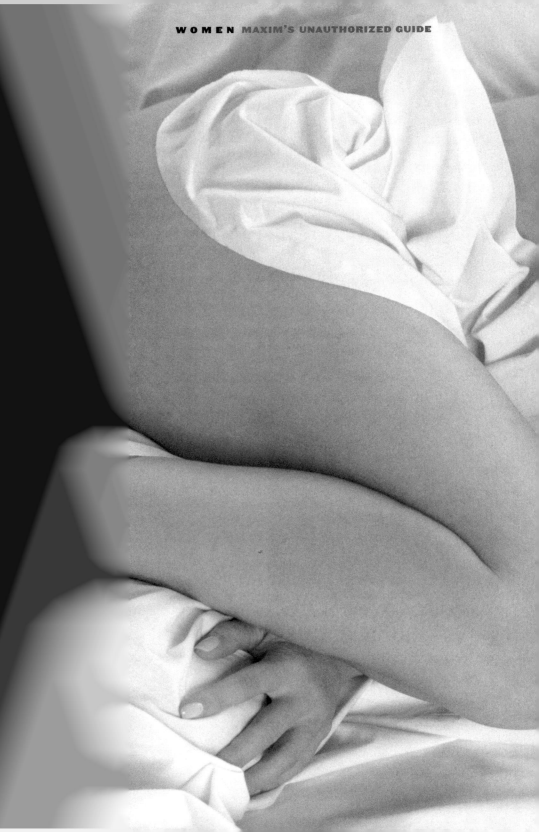

chapter eight

Drive Her Wild

Take her to bed and own her forever.

Throughout the course of this book, the gals and I have shown you how to get beautiful strangers looking your way, how to get them interested in you, how to figure out what they're thinking, what to buy them for their birthdays that'll send just the right message, and a million and one other bits of useful advice. But we're no dummies: We know that at the end of the day what you really want to know is how to get more and better nookie from your little cookie.

The good news is that she wants the same exact thing! Women have tried like hell to keep it a secret, but the fact is, we love a good romp in the hay as much as you. So in this final chapter, we're going to try to refine your technique, teach you some new tricks, get her to experiment in the bedroom, and maybe, if you're very good, even give you the best shot we can at getting you into a threesome. Are you ready? Here's your chance to master the master bedroom by finding out what women want more of...and the most fun ways you can give it to them.

Last Five Minutes LONGER

It takes five minutes for light to travel halfway from the sun, for the blue whale to devour 500 pounds of krill, and for Bill Gates to make $623,000. It also takes the average woman about five minutes longer to reach orgasm than it takes most of you.

Every poll since the Crimean War has shown that one of women's main sexual beefs is that men decant too soon. Experts say that most guys orgasm in less than three minutes (after 30 to 60 thrusts). Most gals require at least seven minutes. Do the math.

But if you'd rather be doing something besides math—and doing it longer—continue reading. We guarantee that by following the advice given, you'll last at least an extra fiver. Hell, if you want, you'll remain hard so long that your erection will need to be carbon-dated.

Learn mind over manhood. The practice most frequently suggested by sex therapists is called the stop-start method, says Mark Schoen, Ph.D., director of sex education at the Sinclair Intimacy Institute in Chapel Hill, North Carolina, and producer of the instructional video *You Can Last Longer: Solutions for Ejaculatory Control* (Sinclair Video Series). You basically rock along until you feel an orgasm rushing on. At that point you freeze, either inside your lover or after you withdraw (she'll probably feel less bereft if you stay inside). Gain control of your senses. Ask yourself what day it is. Give your sausage a moment to cool. Start again. Repeat as needed.

Nothing could be simpler. An orgasm, you see, is one part lust, two parts friction. Stop the friction, stop the orgasm. But here's how to take it to eleven.

To get the most out of the stop-start technique, try to bring yourself closer to the detonation point each time. That way, you'll teach yourself to read the body's signals, to monitor your level of excitement, and to nail the exact millisecond you need to interrupt matters. Over time, experts say, you'll be able to come so darn close to ejaculation—without actually spilling any seed—that you'll almost think you had.

Yet you'll be able to stay erect, and keep on going and going and going, with only an occasional moment's hesitation—perpetually blissful, like some kind of sexual legend.

But will Betty-Lou see you as a Casanova, or as a cad whose constant stopping and starting makes her feel like your sparring partner? "Most women are very supportive. The key is to make sure that the two of you talk about what you're doing and why," says Rohn Friedman, M.D., director of the Human Sexuality Program at Boston's Beth Israel Deaconess Medical Center.

One gal we interviewed indicated she was more than supportive. "I often feel uptight about how long it takes me to climax," says Jodi, 23, a makeup artist in Atlanta. "For my part, alleviating the pressure to climax far outweighed the interruption in stimulation, because it's not like every time my boyfriend stops I go back to ground zero. In fact, it's a lot sexier, because he leaves me hanging—begging, if you want to be honest, which ironically makes me climax faster."

Of course, your teammate doesn't always have to be present for you to practice. Sex experts heartily advise you to take advantage of those tender moments when you're, uh, making love to yourself to practice the stop-start technique.

Press the million-dollar point. You can't see it, but there's an ejaculatory duct down at that low-profile soft spot between the scrotum and the anus (closer to the anus). Press on it as you feel yourself almost ready to spout (firmly for at least three or four seconds) and you will stop the ejaculation. The pressure can be applied with your fingers or hers, or, if you're flexible enough, just about anything, like your heel. (Sit cross-legged atop one heel, and have your sweetheart straddle you, facing frontward or backward.)

The Taoists (pronounced *dow*-ists), who started as devotees of a pro-sex-consciousness-raising movement in China thousands of years ago, call this spot down under the "million-dollar point" (well, that's what it translates into, anyway). Ancient Taoist sexual practices direct men to make great use of their million-dollar point to delay ejaculation for long periods. By so doing, said the ancient Taoists, a man will improve his health and live a long life.

Robert Jaffe, Ph.D., says he's not sure about the long life, but he can vouch that pressing on the right point will delay ejaculation. "Although," adds Jaffe, a family therapist and sex counselor in Encino, California, "most men find the manipulation something of an annoyance." Tony, one 29-year-old guy from Hartford who experimented with digging his heel in, complains that his leg went to sleep in the middle of lovemaking. "But it was a small price to pay for becoming one woman's idol," he modestly confesses.

IF SHE'S HAPPY, NOT ONLY DO YOU GET TO FEEL LIKE A DECENT, COMPASSION-ATE, AND ACCOM-PLISHED HUMAN BEING--YOU'LL GET MORE SEX.

Practice pelvic crunches (a.k.a. penile push-ups). The penis can be trained without the hassle of starting and stopping or pressing your fingers anywhere, says sex therapist and former sex surrogate Anita Banker-Riskin, coauthor (with her husband Michael Riskin, Ph.D.) of *Simultaneous Orgasm & Other Joys of Sexual Intimacy* (Hunter House, 1997). But first you must make the effort to develop your pubococcygeus (PC) muscle, which you're probably now sitting on. The PC muscle involuntarily spasms as you ejaculate, causing semen to fly. But if you purposely contract it during the peak of sex, says Banker-Riskin, the PC muscle acts like the brakes on a car and can bring ejaculation—but not the orgasm!—to a halt.

How do you develop your PC muscle? "Like any other muscle: You exercise it," says Banker-Riskin. But first, you need to identify it. Take a leak and stop the flow without using your hands. Now do that same trick (without actually urinating), and squeeze hard. You just flexed your PC muscle. Hold for one second. Now relax. Repeat. Do a set of 10. Do it once every day. After one week, add another set per day. Build up until you're doing five sets of 10 each day of the week. By that stage, says Banker-Riskin, you will likely notice your new power. Proceed with your sex life, halting ejaculation as you would with the stop-start or press techniques, but by using

10 MOVES GUARANTEED TO MAKE

Former *Maxim* editor Olivia Wolf reveals 10 gal-thrilling techniques that'll melt your girl right off the bed. Because if she's happy, you'll get more sex.

Move #1: Slow it down.
Sex is goal oriented, but lovemaking means savoring every delicious moment. You'd be surprised at how much she enjoys spending hours with you rolling around, mauling each other with your clothes *on*. When you do peel down, do it like an old-fashioned striptease: button by button, layer by layer. Aaah.

Move #2: Kiss us, you fool.
Not just while we're tumbling around during foreplay—throughout the main event, too. Kisses are the ultimate expression of affection and convey an enormous amount of passion. And get her in the game, too: If she's on top and you whisper, "Kiss me," your words will go through her heart like Cupid's arrow, and she'll fall upon your lips like a woman stranded in a desert who's discovered Evian burbling out of the sand. Hand-holding is another gesture that takes on enormous emotional import in bed: When it's

accomplished during actual lovemaking, the feeling is breathtaking.

Move #3: Say our names.
Women appreciate how tough it is to utter anything coherent out of a lust-choked throat. And when it's our name? Wow, that packs a wallop. It reassures her that you're really there, with her and not with some debauched porn-site fantasy. A bit of dirty talking can also be great, but if she laughs, that's your sign that she's just not into it.

Move #4: Press the flesh.
In porn movies, the only body parts making contact are the genitalia. In the real world, we women love it when you cover us like Deion Sanders to maximize skin-on-skin contact. Embrace her in your arms, press her chest against yours, and entwine your arms and legs around her like a meat pretzel. Never push your girl's head down, even if you want her to go there. And when she is going down, for Pete's sake,

don't lie there with your arms folded behind your head like some sleazy Hollywood executive. Run your fingers through her hair, stroke her face, and say something nice, like "Oooohh."

Move #5: Communicate with us.
Women are deathly afraid of sounding like drill sergeants in bed, so give us an easy out by asking (in a whisper is best) if we like what you're doing. Don't break our mood with essay questions—try simple yes-or-no, "Do you want me to do this harder?" queries instead. Likewise, if she's doing something great, let her know with a word or an unambiguous moan of joy.

Move #6: Make us glad we have boobs.
Having breasts is no picnic. Women forfeit the joys of feeling the sun and breeze on their chests at the beach, and bras cost a ton. But in the right man's hands, a woman's boobs can bring her so much pleasure. Don't rush to tear her bra off: Caress and lift the boobage through the

your newly developed mighty PC muscle instead.

Among sex experts, the PC muscle maneuver is a little controversial. James Barada, M.D., director of the Center for Male Sexual Health in Albany, New York, and psychotherapist Jaffe say the Riskin couple may be on to something. Dr. Friedman, however, says that some men find squeezing the PC muscle stimulating, and by squeezing it wind up popping quicker. Only one way to find out.

KISSES ARE THE ULTIMATE EXPRESSION OF AFFECTION AND CONVEY AN ENORMOUS AMOUNT OF PASSION.

Try different strokes. As any Cub Scout who has ever rubbed two sticks together knows, speed and friction make heat. So to turn down the heat, sometimes all you need to do is slow down. "If you want to climax more slowly, move slowly," says sex coach and surrogate Paul Gethard (yes, that's his real name), of Fountain Valley, California. "No heavy thrusting. Just slow, erotic movements."

The ancient Taoists recommended slow, shallow, circular movements to speed up her orgasms while slowing his down. "Going around and around offers maximum stimulation to a woman, because it rubs both her clitoris and the sensitive outer rim

HER SCREAM WITH PLEASURE

material. And handle bare-naked breasts with care. If she's lying on her back, palming them with not much more pressure than the natural weight of your hand feels fantastically manly to a woman, because your hands are so much bigger and heavier than hers. When you kiss her breasts, work your way slowly toward her nipples: While she's actually dying for you to get there, the teasing is an excruciating pleasure.

Move #7: Look us in the eyes.
In bed, looking in her eyes can help you determine how your lover really feels about you. If she quickly looks away, she's not ready to let you get really close. But if she locks your gaze and continues to rock steady, you'll know she's willing to face and share the terror of getting deep into each other. And since you could be ogling her nudity, but are opting instead to look into the windows of her soul, she'll know you're crazy about her, in every sense.

Move #8: Objectify us.
We are not out on the street, where a strange man's unsolicited "Nice

ass, babe!" justifiably elicits an eat-shit-and-die response. Nor are we in a college lecture hall, where the reduction of women to body parts in advertising and art is used to illustrate the oppressive patriarchy. We are in the bedroom, within the context of an intimate exchange, so it's OK to say, "Oh, man, that bra is so sexy," because chances are we put it on that morning hoping for just such a response from you. Remember, women can feel self-conscious in the nude, so say something encouraging, and keep in mind that while "You have a great body" is sweet, specifics resonate more.

Move #9: Let the ladies go first.
If you can manage it, help us to go first. It's no fun taking longer than men to get off. We really have to concentrate, and if we feel like the climax clock is ticking because you've already come and your ministrations are fueled by politeness rather than lust, it's hard for us to stay in the groove. Patience builds intensity, anyway; in the end, you'll probably enjoy your orgasm more if

you've satisfied her first. Give her the racer's edge by engaging in lots of foreplay to bring her close to the brink prior to the main event. Set up a system so your lover can signal just before she blows, and when you get the sign, shift into high gear and join her at the finish.

Move #10: Be a gentleman.
It slays a woman to be pampered and taken care of in bed. If you notice that your gal's head is getting precariously close to the headboard, slip your brawny arm under her and slide her down to safety—then retrieve a pillow and put it under her head. If the covers have fallen off in a chilly bedroom, get on your knees between her legs, pull the blankets up around your shoulders, then gently fall on her, keeping the covers with you. And after the lovin', whatever you do, do not jump up and throw on your pants. (The message that sends: You got what you wanted.) Instead, settle in for some snuggling and a postgame wrap-up (i.e., "I loved it so much when you..."). You're on the road to bliss—if you're not already there.

of the vagina," says George Schiffer, director of the Singing Wind Healing Tao Center in Arlington, Virginia. "It also keeps the man's mind engaged in his gyrations, helping him to last longer." The old Tao masters, says modern Taoist Schiffer, also suggested rhythmically alternating between deep and shallow thrusts. They particularly savored nine shallow followed by one deep.

"The actual rhythm doesn't matter," says Dr. Barada. "As long as you thrust in an alternating fashion, you'll likely slow your ejaculation." And don't worry about boring her with shallow shoves, adds Dr. Barada. He agrees with Schiffer that the outer rim is the place to be. "Most sensation in the vagina is at the entrance, where there is a higher density of nerve endings, not the rear," he says. One 26-year-old office administrator in Holmdel, New Jersey, Carrie, emphatically concurs. "The combination of short and long thrusts is what good sex is all about. The short give the best stimulation, but the long offer an incredibly intimate feeling of being deeply connected. Almost any woman would prefer this thoughtful type of intercourse to mindless pile driving."

Change your mount. Gethard (we swear, we swear...that's really his name) says that the missionary position may build strong triceps, but it often leads to rapid ejaculations. "You get to the point where you're so tired, you just need to ejaculate and collapse," he explains. Try a more relaxed position, he suggests, like spooning—both of you lying on your sides, with her in front. Or flop onto your back, and allow her to straddle you and do all the work.

Dr. Friedman agrees that the female superior position often works better than the missionary, largely because it allows her to do the driving and move in a way that stimulates her. "But," he cautions, "all guys are different." For some men, the

SEX IS GOAL ORIENTED, BUT LOVEMAKING MEANS SAVORING EVERY DELICIOUS MOMENT.

grand view that the woman-on-top provides can make it the most exciting position.

Keep your eyes off the prize. Don't focus on your honey's choicest parts, suggests Banker-Riskin, or the visual stimulation will only move you closer to the edge. If, for example, your most coveted vision is that of Betty Lou's breasts keeping time with the bouncing mattress, try looking into her lovely hazel eyes. If the sight of her dark nether triangle is what makes your juices flow, then raise your sights north of the waistline. If every part of the female anatomy, even Betty Lou's nostrils, drives you wild with lust, then try closing your eyes.

Dress the bishop. Covering Mr. Sunshine in latex is a backseat proven way of lessening penile sensation and prolonging the enjoyably inevitable. But different condoms provide different levels of help, so you'll want to experiment. Dry might be less stimulating than lubricated. Ribbed tend to be thicker (and less stimulating to you) than smooth. Thicker yet are the industrial-strength condoms, such as Ramses Extra and Trojan Extra Strength. Natural skins are the thinnest of all condoms—you'll practically come just slipping them on. (They're also porous and won't protect you against disease.)

Numb your little buddy. They go by such names as Sta-Hard (gel) and Stud 100 (spray). As long as the active ingredient is benzocaine (3 to 7.5 percent in a water-soluble base) or lidocaine (approximately 10 milligrams per spritz), then the product has been approved by the U.S. Food and Drug Administration "for temporary male genital desensitization, helping to slow the onset of ejaculation." These products can in rare cases cause irritation and redness, especially if left on the skin for long. It's best to wash after sex. But don't worry that they'll redden or numb your partner's lining: They won't. "The drug is absorbed into the skin of the penis. You'd have to put on a pretty big glop for it not to be absorbed," says Dr. Barada.

Get expert help. On the off chance that nothing we've said here slows your johnson down, medical doctors can prescribe a cream called EMLA, which is much like the nonprescription desensitizing creams but possibly more effective. "Most doctors will give it to you simply for asking," says Dr. Barada.

And then there are pills: Viagra and beyond. "We've found that certain antidepressant medications, like Zoloft, can prolong erections," says Dr. Barada. The medications are given in small doses, and they're given intermittently, not long-term. The main side effect of these drugs is fatigue, and typically they would be prescribed for men suffering from clinical premature ejaculation as opposed to mattress cowboys looking to improve their already respectable saddle time. But it can't hurt to ask.

Class dismissed...prepare to be worshiped.

Women Spill the Moves
That Make 'Em Melt

"I like it when a guy leaves your clothes on while you're messing around. Don't take them off—work around them. Move your hands inside my bra without ripping it off or unhooking it. Guys love to be free and naked of their pants and just want to get right to it, no inhibiting factors. But most women I know want guys to work at it, make it mysterious—rub their hands over your clothes, like a high school flashback. We need a little time to fantasize to get really hot. But I still want him to be the one to undress me: It's sexier." —Angie, 26, assistant producer, New York City

"That kiss: the one where they take both hands and cradle your face, thumbs over the ears, pinkies under the chin, and pull you to them and lay a kiss on you like that. That is so amazing, like they *really* want you. That's a weak-knee kiss, guaranteed." —Judy, 30, engineer, Peoria, Illinois

"I love to be stroked all over when I'm first waking up. Slide your hands over my breasts, down my stomach, up my thighs. But don't touch me down there yet—wait until I get so excited that I can't stand it anymore. That guarantees that I'll be wet enough to facilitate—and intensify—further action." —Jade, 25, playwright, Berkeley, California

IN BED, LOOKING IN HER EYES CAN HELP YOU DETERMINE HOW YOUR LOVER REALLY FEELS ABOUT YOU.

"Go slow, slow, slow...*then* fast. Starting out too quickly just makes me think he's rushing it from the get go, and I can't get beyond that and relax and enjoy myself." —Maggie, 23, editorial assistant, Garden City, New York

"I don't think men understand how much women love requests to wear certain articles of clothing. Like if there's a bathrobe or some special underwear he says is really sexy, it's very sexy for *us* to wear it for him." —Alicia, 32, paramedic, Rome, New York

"Sometimes when my guy and I are screwing, he'll just stop when he's all the way inside me, and we'll take a rest and let all the sensations rush over us without disconnecting. It's way hotter than pounding away endlessly." —Lucy, 29, lawyer, Clifton, New Jersey

"I hadn't seen this guy for three weeks, and when we got into bed, he immediately went down on me. But before he did, he said, 'I've been thinking about doing this for three weeks.' For some reason, women are never convinced that guys actually enjoy going down on them, so his saying that was a tremendous psychological turn-on." —Vicki, 35, doctor, Erie, Pennsylvania

"I like it when a guy demonstrates that he's absorbed the best of both genders' sexual styles. For example, he'll move really slowly and kiss you really lightly, but then swoop you off the couch and carry you into the bedroom, throw you down and manhandle you (but not in a scary way). Then when he reaches your most delicate parts he's back to Mr. Gentle. It just shows he understands—and can manipulate—the variety of things I love during sex!" —Christina, 29, publicist, Miami

HER BEST SEX EVER

You wanted to know, so we called a bunch of the girls and asked: What was your best sex ever? If these tales don't inspire you, you should think about the priesthood.

Sneaky Sex

"One time I sneaked into this guy's room just wearing garters and stockings and high heels. It was very secretive and we never even turned the lights on—no one in the house was supposed to know we were having sex because we were all friends and our relationship was just starting. I just walked in and was like *hello*. The furtiveness and secretiveness of it all made it incredible." —Carrie, 24, graduate student, Phoenix

Island Hopping

"The best sex I ever had was on a tiny deserted island in the Caribbean with a guy I barely knew. We found a five-star resort that wasn't opening for another week and asked for a room. We were the only guests in the resort, at the pool, in the restaurant, on their private beach. That afternoon we had sex that went on for hours that we both remember for different reasons. I remember it because it was the only time that someone has made me have such an amazing orgasm that I lost complete control and burst into tears. He remembers it because we bumped and thrashed around so much that we moved the bed all the way across to the other side of the room without noticing. I guess it was a good thing there were no guests next door!" —Sue, 25, sales representative, Cincinnati

Cosmic Connection

"My best sex? It had to be the guy I dated when I was new to sex; he made me feel as if he and I were one with the cosmos when we were in bed together. It was pretty incredible. Unfortunately, I have no idea how he did this. He had long hair and a beard, and he believed in the healing power of crystals—it all sounds pretty laughable except that sex with him was so awesome! Perhaps he got my chakras in line. Or more likely it was because he treated me like an ancient earth goddess, and my body as a sacred temple. Whatever he did, it worked!" —Jolie, 29, librarian, Philadelphia

Private Party, Please!

"The best sex for me is when you feel like the guy you're in love with is as into it as you are at that very moment. Once, when I was at a party at my boyfriend's apartment, I saw him across the room and felt like I just had to have him. So I went over to him and I think he kissed me and whispered something in my ear, and then we both just sort of gravitated toward his room. We went in, closed the door, and had sex right there with more than 50 people in the other room. No amount of technical prowess can match the feeling of really wanting to have sex with your man and then getting it." —Tara, 26, teacher, Seattle

Frisky Friend-Fling

"It was with a casual friend whom I'd been flirting with for months. We both knew why we were there, so there were no worries that it would ruin our friendship. He was also younger and more inexperienced, so he didn't try to impress me with misguided attempts; he stuck with what he knew, and just the basics were plenty. Sometimes guys go through all the foreplay motions in set order (kiss, shirt, bra, panties) and you don't even notice it; it's like they're reading along to some invisible set of instructions as they go. But he took his time, and I could tell he was enjoying every step, which made me like the whole thing more. There was no pressure or expectation—it was the perfect night." —Kara, 23, writer, Tulsa

Dirty Day-Trippers

"My best time was when my boyfriend and I checked into a hotel right near where we lived. We spent the entire day just fooling around, walking around naked, and having sex. No rush, no worries—it was just about the two of us. It was the perfect way to waste a day." —Serena, 26, advertising executive, Boston

G-Spot Gee Whiz!

"The best sex I ever had was right after I had broken up with my long-term boyfriend. I had just started seeing this other guy and was pretty nervous because I had never been with anyone else. Well, we were fooling around and he discovered my G-spot. I had no idea I had one, and I couldn't stop giggling because it felt so good. So I'm laughing nonstop for about 10 minutes and then he started laughing and then we had amazing sex. I think it was so good because he made it seem like my pleasure was just as important as his—that I could take as long as I needed to and not feel pressured to come." —Arabella, 25, medical student, Cambridge, Massachusetts

Ask Her Anything!!!

Real women answer your most pressing flesh-pressing questions.

1. Does size matter? Be honest.

"Not really. Well, I've never thought anyone was too small. This sounds corny, but it's really what you make of it." —Lisa, 23, student, New York City

"It does, but not that much. You can feel the difference, but after the initial thrust, technique wins over size. And any guy who is talented with his tongue will make me forget all about how small he might be!" —Josie, 26, social worker, Stamford, Connecticut

"Yes, because you can't feel it if it's not big enough. I have experienced the smallness, and it's no experience at all. There's a certain amount of technique that can make up for the size, but nothing can completely replace it." —Lori, 24, photographer, Las Vegas, Nevada

"Yes. I always thought I was a size-doesn't-matter kind of girl, but then I hopped into bed with a guy who had a little penis. I almost laughed. It wasn't miniscule; it just seemed out of proportion to this hunky guy. However, I didn't find that it made a difference when it came to intercourse; it pretty much felt like others I'd been with. As far as big penises are concerned, I'm not into a huge one. I hooked up with a guy but didn't sleep with him because the sight of his 'thang' was so scary, I didn't know what I would do with it. It certainly wouldn't fit inside me." —Courtney, 25, legal assistant, New Orleans

The bottom line: Size does matter, but maybe not as much as you think. If it's more than about three inches erect, it's probably not worth wasting your energy obsessing about it; the more self-conscious you are about it, the more she'll pick up on it. As most women pointed out, it's creativity over size almost every time, so a small size just means you've gotta really master the techniques. Please read this chapter three times.

2. Does anal sex do anything for you, or do you just do it to please guys?

"The first time I did it, it was all for me. I was fooling around with my boyfriend and he was rubbing his fingers all over 'down there,' and it started to feel really good in the area a little, well, farther back. So I encouraged him, and he started doing the anal probe with his fingers. It was feeling really, really good, so I told him to go ahead and try the whole shebang. It was pretty shocking at first, a tiny bit painful, but still pretty good. Then I did it with another guy, and he kept hinting at it every time we got in bed and I ended up doing it to make him happy. He did it for too long and too hard, and I lost that feel-good feeling for myself. So, yes, anal sex can be good for women, but she's got to have the control." —Anna, 29, college professor, Milwaukee

"You can't do rough and crazy anal sex that just pleases a guy. That's not fun. It's got to be gentle and slow and *all about her*." —Lisa, 30, waitress, Eugene, Oregon

"Three words: lubrication, lubrication, lubrication. It feels kind of funny—a mixture of pleasure and pain. Not all bad if the guy takes it easy and listens to what I have to say." —Lynne, 25, model, New York City

The bottom line: There are women out there who like anal sex. But no chick outside a John Holmes flick wants to be banged back there with complete abandon. Make sure you pay attention to what she says—after all, you want her to want to do it again, right?

3. If your boyfriend offered you an hourlong massage in exchange for a blow job, would you think he was a jerk and get pissed off?

"I hate giving massages and I like getting them, so I think that would be a pretty good exchange. I certainly wouldn't get pissed off." —Miranda, 24, chef, New Haven, Connecticut

"Bring it on! For an hourlong massage I'd give him two! If that would make him knead my flesh for more than five minutes, I'd do anything. And if you added oil and candles, I'd...well, who knows!" —Amy, 23, reporter, Atlanta

"I would think he was an angel sent from heaven. The way I see it, an hour is an hour. If I could get a man to spend an hour rubbing my body without the drooling fourth-grade fondling where he's only doing it to get me hot for sex, that would be great. Which is why I'd blow him first so the temptation would be gone and he would be massaging purely for my benefit. That would be awesome." —Lara, 28, singer, Nashville

"It sounds like the kind of thing that you can negotiate if you've been going out for a while and are comfortable 'bargaining' in your sex life. If I'd been seeing a guy only a few weeks, I would wig if he said, 'Hey, back rub for a blow job?'" —Rachel, 29, writer, New York City

The bottom line: Break out the oil. Pretty much every woman we asked seemed to love this trade. Just don't skimp on our massages...we know you'll want the full lickathon, too.

4. What's the one *simple* thing a guy can do to get you to shag him more?

"Let *me* come up with the idea first." —Allison, 23, editorial assistant, New York City

"All I ask is that he's clean and tastes good. There's nothing

HAND-HOLDING IS AN EASY GESTURE THAT TAKES ON ENORMOUS EMOTIONAL IMPORT IN BED.

HOW TO SPOT A FAKE ORGASM

It looked real. It sounded real. It felt real. But did she...really? Six telltale signs that bliss is bogus.

There's no flush. During orgasm, blood flow increases and becomes more apparent on the skin's surface. Look for a light, rashlike crimson glow creeping across your honey's cheeks and chest immediately after she goes all wobbly. It's easy to detect—in the light, at least. And according to Bernie Zilbergeld, Ph.D., author of *The New Male Sexuality* (Bantam Doubleday Dell, 1999), "the sex flush is the only sign a woman can't fake."

She's too dramatic. Remember the "I'll have what she's having" restaurant scene in *When Harry Met Sally*? Be skeptical of the big-screen effort, but don't interrupt the performance: Sex therapist Barbara Keesling, Ph.D., author of *Super Sexual Orgasm* (HarperCollins, 1997), warns, "She may be exciting herself with her own sound effects."

She doesn't look stoned. At the big moment, her pupils will dilate, according to Beverly Whipple, Ph.D., renowned female-orgasm authority and associate professor at Rutgers University. "Her sympathetic nervous system is activated, which increases pupil diameter," Whipple says.

There's no panting. At the euphoric end, her blood pressure will rise (sometimes by 50 percent), and her heart and breathing rates will increase significantly, too. How to test her vitals? Put your hand on her chest...er, heart.

No clench. The clench is the clincher. When she's really coming, the vaginal muscles will clench and grip in a rapid-fire succession; sexperts Masters and Johnson estimate that the muscles contract more than once per second.

Exquisite timing. If you two are in perfect O sync, be skeptical. According to *The Hite Report*'s much-quoted survey of 3,000 women, only 30 percent said they reached cloud nine regularly during intercourse. So if your little lady comes real quickly, comes exactly when you do, and comes every time, she's probably faking. (If she passes all of the above tests, immediately send her address to: Male Editors, *Maxim*, 1040 Avenue of the Americas, New York, NY 10018, so we can contact her for future scientific research.)

sexier than a man who's freshly showered, with wet hair and a towel around his waist." —Joanna, 27, college administrator, Allentown, Pennsylvania

"Take me out somewhere very public but where we can still dance or touch each other. It builds up the suspense and makes me feel more special than if he just drops by with a video and a pizza." —Suzanne, 33, surgeon, Grand Rapids

"Be more active. I once dated a lazy shit who would just sit around and watch MTV with a bag of Doritos and then want to have sex. Blech. My last boyfriend was a little sportier and played soccer. When he came home with a damp, sweaty shirt, all worn out: yum. He earned me." —Mandi, 26, legal assistant, Lindenhurst, New York

The bottom line: So, to recap, have a life, let her lead sometimes, shower frequently, and take her out for a bit. That's not so bad, eh?

5. If you fantasize during sex or alone when you masturbate, what do you fantasize about?

"I usually fantasize about guys I want to have sex with. Sometimes movie stars (that's so silly, I know, but you see a good Johnny Depp movie...), but more often it's guys I've met, guys from work, guy friends—whoever I've most recently found myself looking at in a sexy way. I've definitely done the fantasy thing about a guy when I'm with another guy—which men don't want to hear—but I'm sure they do it, too." —Gwen, 26, showroom manager, Los Angeles

"When I'm alone, I think about domination with some guy I know, sort of pretending my hands and feet are tied up or something. It spices it up." —Melanie,

30, accounts manager, Redding, Pennsylvania

"My fantasies when I touch myself alone are usually about women, maybe because then I'm focusing on my own female form. They're pretty weird, like I'm the cheerleading coach and one of the girls digs me, or it's college and some hot female professor takes advantage of me. But I'm totally normal other than that, really! If I'm with a guy, I usually just think about being tied up—unless I'm already tied up!" —Carolyn, 29, actuary, Stamford, Connecticut

"I don't usually fantasize during sex—usually I'm focused on the person I'm with or just on how it feels. Thinking about someone else is a distraction. But I do like to fantasize while I'm on a long bus ride or a plane, and then I think about a stranger coming up to me and just ravishing me on the spot. Just to be with someone without knowing anything about them, being able to be completely uninhibited—that would be ideal." —Sherri, 24, flight attendant, Queens, New York

"This sounds a little disturbing, but when I masturbate I tend to think about being held against my will—like I'm in a harem and the sheik has decided it's my turn tonight. Or he has ordered the other harem women to touch me all over while he watches from behind a screen. In real life, I would never want to be forced into anything, but it makes for good fantasy." —Darlene, 25, financial analyst, Chicago

The bottom line: Well, you certainly don't need to feel guilty about *your* fantasies, since her imagination works overtime, too. A number of women said they fantasized to hurry their orgasms up, so make sure to ask her about her secret fantasies, and maybe you can make them come to life—and make sex more fun for both of you.

How to Praise Her Private Parts

She's got a great rack. But blurting out "Those titties are tremendous" will guarantee you never lay eyes on her nipples again. If you do manage to compliment her special assets properly, it can be a huge turn-on for her. Try these tips from real women.

> IN THE RIGHT MAN'S HANDS, A WOMAN'S BOOBS CAN BRING HER SO MUCH PLEASURE.

"I've always been self-conscious about my small breasts, and most men never say anything about them, which makes it even worse. But recently this guy I'm dating told me that my breasts look like they're out of a painting in a museum—so delicate and beautiful. It was the first time he'd ever seen me naked, and it made me much more excited about going to bed with him." —Anne, 26, creative consultant, Omaha

"I'm not sure what guys should say, but I know what they shouldn't say: 'Your labia is so perfect,' or it's so pink, or it's so tight, or it's so, well, whatever; it all sounds absolutely schmucky and stupid. I say don't go there." —Andrea, 27, producer, Irvington, New York

"One guy told me that my you-know-what was the pinkest he'd ever seen—and I took that as a compliment. Telling a woman she has pretty private parts is a nice thing to do, but make sure it doesn't sound like you've seen and scrutinized a million others!" —Beth, 21, property management assistant, Des Moines, Iowa

"'God, I love your breasts' is acceptable, especially if she's self-conscious about them. One guy I dated used to say 'Nice ass' in a really lecherous way, which I must admit I loved." —Jordana, 20, student, Bismarck, North Dakota

"You don't always have to say something to show you like it. All you have to do is pay extra attention to that particular body part. Don't stare at my breasts all day— just spend some time there when we're in bed, and I'll get the compliment that way." —Amanda, 24, speech pathologist, Oakland, California

"I never mind when people say I have a great ass." —Cindy, 25, social worker, Bronx, New York

"You can be less graphic by just saying, 'You have gorgeous curves,' or 'You're so beautiful *everywhere*.' And I love being told my body parts are soft." —Donna, 24, receptionist, Boston

"When I was younger, I did worry about whether I looked different down there than other women, and I remember my boyfriend saying I looked like 'a delicate little flower.' It sounded dorky, so we both laughed, but it was the sweetest compliment, and I felt really comfortable, um, opening up to him in the future." —Gina, 30, high school teacher, Fairfield, Connecticut

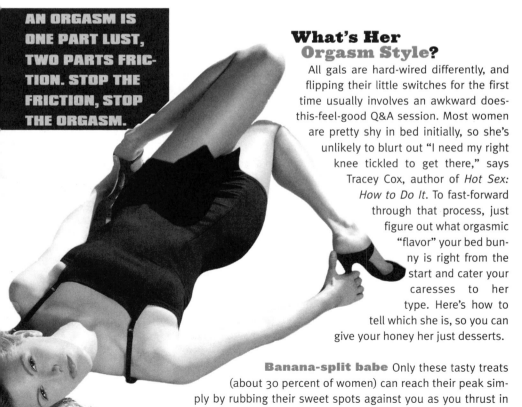

AN ORGASM IS ONE PART LUST, TWO PARTS FRICTION. STOP THE FRICTION, STOP THE ORGASM.

What's Her Orgasm Style?

All gals are hard-wired differently, and flipping their little switches for the first time usually involves an awkward does-this-feel-good Q&A session. Most women are pretty shy in bed initially, so she's unlikely to blurt out "I need my right knee tickled to get there," says Tracey Cox, author of *Hot Sex: How to Do It*. To fast-forward through that process, just figure out what orgasmic "flavor" your bed bunny is right from the start and cater your caresses to her type. Here's how to tell which she is, so you can give your honey her just desserts.

Banana-split babe Only these tasty treats (about 30 percent of women) can reach their peak simply by rubbing their sweet spots against you as you thrust in and out; the rest need a little help.

How to tell if she's this type: First, assume she's *not* this easy-breezy type. If you assume she is and she ain't, and you turn into a human pumping machine too soon without giving her the stimulation she needs (with your fingers or your mouth), she'll either be convinced that a) you're a selfish bastard, or b) your last girlfriend could orgasm effortlessly through intercourse only and you'll be disappointed that she can't, or c) she'll be forgiving but then, after *you* finish, she'll have to go through that awkwardness of saying, "Um, Mayday, the eagle *hasn't* landed—can I get some lovin' over here?"

Second, look for the signs. If you're stimulating her manually or orally and she seems to get really close and then stops you or squirms away, she may already be halfway to the big Olé. If she's breathing heavy, is very wet and starts pulling you toward her (or clawing the top of the nightstand for the condom), she probably wants you to get in there, slugger. At this point ask her if she wants to take the reins. "It's much easier to orgasm—particularly the first time with a new guy—if I'm on top, because then I have more control over what speed and how hard I grind myself against him," says Faye, 26, a music publicist in Nashville.

Finally, if all the signs indicate you're under the sheets with a banana-split type, double-check by asking, incredulously, "Can you [pause] 'get there' with me inside of you?" If she says no, you can always back-pedal casually by adding, "Yeah, that's totally rare, isn't it? I want you to go first...what do you like?"

How to up the ante: If you're with this type of woman, the next rung on the sexual ladder is, of course, simultaneous orgasm. You'll need to do three things. First, tell her that you want to try and achieve simultaneous pleasure (she'll love that you're the kind of guy who wants to make sex better and better). Second, give her a head start—get her almost there through other stimulation before you ever, um, let your rabbit into the burrow. Third, look into her eyes—most women will say, "Now, God, yes, now" to let you know the magic time has come; but if she's a quiet babe, you'll need to look for nonverbal clues in her facial expression. (Same thing if she's screaming like a banshee and gouging fingernail furrows into your back.)

Strawberry-shortcake sweetie Most women fall into this category (55 to 60 percent of women). They can definitely go to the moon, but not via your rocket alone: They need an assist from your fingers or your tongue.

How to tell if she's this type: Look for the following signs. First, she may avoid stroking you or getting you too excited, because she's assuming she's going first and if she gets you overexcited she'll feel pressure to hurry, when what she needs to feel is relaxed. Second, when you touch her with your fingers or your tongue, she settles into a position and doesn't pull back when things heat up. "I try to let a new guy know that the foreplay of him touching my clitoris is actually my main course by just saying, 'Don't stop—keep going,'" explains Mel, 30, an animal trainer in San Diego. "But some guys actually think it's cute to stop and tease me. That's fine if we've been together many times, but early on, 'Don't stop' is a real direction that should be followed."

ONE OF WOMEN'S MAIN SEXUAL BEEFS IS THAT MEN DECANT TOO SOON.

If the signs seem right, double-check to see if she's this type by saying—as she's getting into it but before the "Don't stop!" stage—"I want to make you come" (or "orgasm" or "make it happen for you," whatever seems natural to you). If she's a strawberry shortcake and wants the big O, she'll signal a desire to keep up the foreplay. (Banana splits will indicate they want to move on to sex; nonorgasmic vanilla sundaes will find a way to tell you not to worry about their orgasms.)

How to up the ante: The next step after being able to make her orgasm through manual or oral stimulation is to coax her into banana-split city. Once you've discovered the style she responds to—a light or heavy touch, fast or slow—you can suggest trying to see if *you can help her* orgasm while you're inside her. (The you-can-help-her part is crucial because you want to put the pressure on yourself, and not turn it into some sort of sex challenge for her.) Then, ask her to tell you when she's at the brink—she probably won't get as much stimulation once you're inside her, so wait to enter until she's almost at the pearly gates. You may need to give her a hand or get a little creative, but stay focused and you'll be able to send her over the edge with ease. "I've only been able to climax during intercourse with one man," says Margaret, 27, a fund-raiser in Washington, D.C. "It was because he could stop, pull out, rub me with his fingers, go back in, stop, more rubbing. He had great control and was willing to do this combo move so that we could have that intimacy of me coming while he was inside me."

Vanilla sundae Is she a vanilla sundae who, like 10 to 15 percent of women, hasn't ever hit the big O and learned just how flavorful the world can truly be?

How to tell if she's this type: Here's your big chance to make her personal history book. Every woman remembers the first guy who made her orgasm—because many women have sex a few times, or a few dozen times, without orgasm until they find the right, patient guy to guide them through nature's little wonder. "Sure, I remember the guy I lost my virginity to at 17, but I remember with great fondness, respect, and lust the more experienced guy who helped me orgasm for the first time, at 21," says Jennifer, 31, a teacher in Charlotte, North Carolina. "He puts all those other guys—who'd been too lazy or inconsiderate to deal with my naiveté—to shame."

What are the signs that she's never been to the land of O? Watch out if she seems in a hurry to get to your main event without worrying about her own pleasure. Being extremely shy about saying what she likes or wants in bed, even after you gently coax her a few times, is another sign. You don't want to embarrass her by accusing, "Haven't you ever had an orgasm before?" A nicer question to ask is, "I want to make you feel good. Is there a way you touch yourself that feels good?" (This is a good moment to make sure she's over 18.) This question will help you figure out if she can climax alone but hasn't with a partner before. If that's the case, ask her to tell you—better yet, show you—what she does when she's solo.

How to up the ante: If she's never met Mr. O, it could be that she's never explored herself properly. You can help: Move a finger around gently until she registers a new and encouraging tingle, and then proceed from there.

It may take a few times to get her there, but make sure not to push her. If she's really having trouble, it could be something psychological that's blocking her bliss. But if she just hasn't found the right touch for her (not every woman has three vibrators, despite what your porn movies have taught you) and you're the one who helps your gal have her first sighting of God, most states require that she become your love slave for life.

Going Downtown

Bill Clinton may not consider oral sex "real" sex, but most women do. In fact, when a woman is on the receiving end of a man's oral attention, oral sex is more than just real sex—it's really, really amazing sex. You see, inch for inch, the muscle in your mouth holds more potential for a woman's pleasure than the one in your pants. Your limber lingua can deftly reach those little spots where the Big Guy can't go. And that makes all the difference.

"In college I had boyfriends who went down on me, and I was like, I don't get it. So I thought it was me that had the problem, not them," recalls Cindy, 25, a social worker in Bronx, New York. "Then after college I met a man who went down, and

---

MÉNAGE À MAYBE

The Mile High Club's for rookies: If you want true sex-god status, you've gotta wrangle your way into the ultra-exclusive Threesome Club. Former *Maxim* editor Nancy Miller recounts her own close encounters of the third kind and gives you the password.

We are watching Catherine Deneuve run her tongue along the tender thigh of Susan Sarandon when my boyfriend cavalierly brings up The Subject, pretending it's just come to him: "Hey—uh, you've never slept with a woman, have you?" Here we go again. I have seen *The Hunger* with my past two boyfriends, and when Deneuve, the bloodthirsty vampiress, performs a soft-focus seduction on Sarandon to the choral strains of Debussy, this conversation must always surface. "Nope," I say. There's a beat while the two undead lesbos writhe around on the bed. "Would you ever, like, uh, maybe, like, be into..." (Oh, just say it, you weenie.) "Be into what?" I ask with obviously feigned ignorance. "You know—uh, a ménage à trois." Smiling, I look at him and say, "Well-I-I-I...maybe...but I don't know..."

Yes, I am torturing him, just as you are probably tortured by all the near-epic tales you hear of ménages, the stories that drive you to gaze at the heavens and cry, "Why doesn't that shit ever happen to me?"

The good news, according to the pros at the Kinsey Institute, is that there is a 50 percent chance that the woman you're with may quite sincerely be interested in someday forming

179

things were...different. This man had skills. All of a sudden, the heavens opened up, and I was like, *Holy shit. This is the best thing that ever happened to me.* I even ran home the next morning and spilled to my friends how amazing he was."

If you're a guy who *really* knows how to go down on a woman, just "good in bed" won't describe you. "Perfect man" or "blessed by the gods" might be more like it. Here's how to get there.

> **YOU'LL PROBABLY ENJOY YOUR ORGASM MORE IF YOU'VE SATISFIED HER FIRST.**

1. Give great lip service. Thanks to the "not so fresh" mythology, we think that 10 minutes of oral sex is like six months on a chain gang to you, and a lot of women worry that guys go down on them just to help keep the sex train rolling. To assure us that you don't buy into all that nonsense, layer it on extra thick just how much you dig heading downtown. Before you've undone the last button of her Levi's, whisper in her ear how every inch of her turns you on and that it would be like Christmas morning for you if she'd let you give her some big ol' kisses down there. "When a guy tells me how excited he is to go down on me, it lets me know that he's not just doing it as par for the course," says Denise, 28, a computer programmer in Memphis. "I can relax and get ready to enjoy myself."

2. Survey the land with your hand. In a matter of minutes, you're going

MÉNAGE À MAYBE

a human triangle. And I suspect that's a conservative estimate. The bad news? Even if your pro-ménage madam is 100 percent into a trio, one or two insensitive pressure moves on your part can guarantee she'll hold off until after she's dumped you and found someone more tactful. If you want your hot fantasy to come true, you're going to have to play it cool.

Insight #1: **Don't push the issue.** After my boyfriend (let's call him Fred...because that's his name) got finished asking me questions, I asked him one: "So...do you want us to have a ménage?" His answer: "Yeah! It'd be really hot!" Can't say Fred doesn't speak his mind.

But speaking your mind may be the last thing to do if you want to make your dream a reality. Personally, I like a man who acts nonchalant. A guy who says something like: "Well, if it happens, it happens...but if it doesn't, no big deal." Pow! You've just upped your ménage potential tenfold. And that's not just my opinion. "The guy who keeps pushing the three-way comes off creepy, not sexy," explains Marie, a single friend of mine who,

though intrigued by the idea of sex with women, is wary of ménage hounds. "The guy who doesn't seem to care that much is the one I am more likely to sock it to."

Insight #2: **Your girlfriend can't feel like a third wheel.** From that point on, life went on normally for Fred and me, except that he would often put a third potato in the oven (he had subconsciously started buying everything in threes) when there was only the two of us for dinner. And, of course, The Subject came up with enough frequency for me to start worrying: Am I boring in bed? Is that why he wants another woman? Because I'm such a bad lay, he needs to double up?

See, even if your woman is sexually curious, if you suggest another partner—especially if you suggest it more than once—she'll instantly suspect you're trying to tell her she's not hot enough. Imagine it the other way: "Hey, sweets," your partner says to you, "I love you and everything, but let's make our relationship better by having you and another man do me next Saturday." Bet you wouldn't be so into to be dispatched on a pleasure mission with no flashlight, no map, and a 50 percent decrease in oxygen because there's a blanket over your head. Did I mention it's (at least) 98.6 degrees under there? So get a grip on her bod beforehand. While you're kissing her neck and cooing in her ear, slide your fingers slowly down her body. Make a rest stop at her chest and do a few slow laps around each breast with your fingers. Be lazy. Take your time. A series of pit stops that tickle and tease will get her plenty buttered up before you even get there, and with each relaxed breath, she'll let herself go in the trusted hands (and soon, the mouth) of a pro.

Once your fingers have reached the Promised Land, take a moment and gather yourself. A woman's private bits are carefully tucked away and covered in lace undies for a reason: They're delicate. So don't go rooting around as if you're trying to dig quarters out of a bowl of change. Approach her precious parts like a blind millionaire reading his bank statement in Braille. Lightly, carefully, gingerly glide your fingers across the outside, uh, petals. Using your first two fingers, gently—and I mean gently—stroke her and gradually work your way inside the petals, making sure you glide around—not on—that little button full of nerve endings that *rhymes with Dolores,* as Seinfeld would say. Circle your two fingers softly, stimulating her while you survey the area, getting a sense of where she likes to be touched and how. Inevitably, if you're tender enough, Dolores might pop out. That's her body's

sharing then.

The other thing that happens when a guy is being a ménage à pest is that it forces the woman to think about the actual act more than she wants to. Sure, women are beautiful, but do I really want to do one? The thought of kissing a girl is OK, touching a boob I can get into, but the idea of putting my fingers (or mouth—yikes!) in certain strangely familiar pockets gives me pause. I wouldn't mind putting my feet up and kicking back while my boyfriend and some gorgeous woman ravished me all night. But when it came time to pay the piperette, I might find myself a little short of change. And the more you hammer me about the subject, the more time I'm going to spend thinking about it and getting creeped out.

My friend Monica recalls her perfect ménage experience, with her boyfriend, Jeff, and her best friend, Karen: "We were all at my mother's beach house, enjoying a little too much wine. Then Karen and I went out on the deck and jumped into the hot tub. We got naked and were just hanging out, and there was definite sexual tension between us. When my boyfriend jumped into the hot tub, he was like the catalyst that got things rolling, even though he didn't do anything overt. I reached over to the both of them, and it was, like, Hello. Pretty soon we were all just touching each other, never minding who was who." Monica claims that the lack of planning meant there were no expectations. "Jeff and I had never talked about it, so I knew I didn't have to do anything I didn't want to way of playing *The Price Is Right*—i.e., yelling, "Come on down!"

3. Let the games begin. Now that you've "marked" your territory with your fingers, use the same scenic route with your mouth that you took with your hands. Kiss, lick, nibble all the places you touched before as a proper way of saying, "Allow me, once again, to introduce myself." Don't rush—she'll think you can't wait to come up for air—but don't bandy about either; you want to keep her moving steadily toward the goal.

Before you plant your face in there like you're bobbing for apples, let's reflect a moment on the Zen principles of oral pleasure. You can't "see" pleasure in a woman, but you can feel it. With your tongue, trace the contours inside and outside just as you did with your fingers. Then square your jaw and move inside with your tongue and lips. Now give her a light smooch. Then a long, lingering kiss, then a swirly doopity doop with your tongue. Feel familiar? That's right, you're kissing her, with all the sensuality of your lips and the seductive probing with your tongue that you use when you kiss her on her mouth.

Again, easy does it. Think of your technique more like tasting an ice cream cone, or trying to eat a bowl of very hot soup, or tracing her name in cursive, or catching a snowflake on your tongue. Try a bunch of different things to give her a selection to choose from. (Bush-league techniques that don't work: "hummingbird" rapid tongue

do." Because Jeff hadn't nagged her, Monica didn't feel she had to really get down with this woman or later hear her boyfriend's anguished "That was our big chance, and you didn't get down!"

Insight #3: It's best to let it happen naturally. For all the reasons stated above, even the most inquisitive females' ménage fantasies require one tricky condition: "I only want it if it happens spontaneously." To you, that's like expecting to win the lottery without buying a ticket. With a third person as a necessary ingredient, how do you get it to happen spontaneously? This is the hardest part for men to understand: You don't. (Sucks, huh?) But that's the way it is: Though you may be dying to grab your girlfriend's address book and start plowing into possibilities, your girlfriend, most likely, would prefer that you left it alone and waited it out until a potential situation arrives. And when the beautiful constellation comes together, which it can, if you let it...

Witness Greg's blissful backseat ride: "My girlfriend and I were drinking screwdrivers in the back of my Chevy Impala with her best friend, waiting on my friend Peter, who was supposed to double-date with us. He never showed, but while we waited, my girlfriend and I started kissing and fooling around a little. But we felt bad—OK, she felt bad—because this other girl was all by herself. At one point my girlfriend started kind of caressing her, and then I started caressing her, and she didn't have any reluctance at all, and I started thinking, Hey, maybe...

"The next thing I knew, they were both getting undressed together, and I was sitting there in amazement, drinking and watching them. At first I'm thinking, This is the best show I've ever seen. Then I'm thinking, If I don't get in there quick, they're gonna kick me out and send me home. So I joined them.

"My mind was racing the whole time. You can't pay attention to two girls at once: You have to shift your attention back and forth, like a tennis match. The risk of overstimulation is high, and I wanted to, um, stay with it as long action, deep tongue lunges, anything involving teeth.) As she gets more into it, you can gently slide a finger or two in there—but keep your mouth up and around Dolores' neighborhood.

4. Love her…don't leave her. Sometimes when a guy focuses so much on going down on a woman, she starts to feel like the magician's assistant who's been put in a box and sawed in half. She's lying there, looking around as the guy's solely fixated on her bottom half. "I've had guys go down on me and it's like they disappear," says Maureen, 26, an elementary school teacher in Brooklyn, New York. "It makes you want to lift the blanket and shout, 'Hello? Are you OK down there?'"

It can get a little cold and lonely when you're gone. So guys, quell her Bermuda Triangle phobia by giving her a three-minute demo of your work—then pay a 30-second visit back upstairs to check quality control. Smile and say, "I'm really enjoying this. Is there something that you really like that I'm doing/can do?" This gives her the chance to put in a special request for a tongue ripple or for you to put your fingers inside of her. When you head south again, don't hold back your excitement. Moan in pleasure as you give her hips a good squeeze, caress her belly and breasts, and kiss the inside of her thighs.

---

as possible; so I spent a lot of time with foreplay. But when we did get around to actual intercourse, they started to get a little catty."

Insight #4: Make it clear to whichever one you're going home with that she's number one. Trying to please two women simultaneously is like being a D.J. spinning two tables—and if one of those tables is your main squeeze, you'd better make sure you never let her forget that. Continues Greg: "I started having real sex with the new girl first, and my girlfriend actually guided me in; but I started to get a little too involved, and my girlfriend got clingy and uptight, saying, 'OK, now it's my turn.'"

"Making the girlfriend of primary importance is crucial to most successful ménages," explains Ted McIlvenna, Ph.D., who heads the Institute for the Advanced Study of Human Sexuality in San Francisco. The first time the three of you meet, sex experts suggest, try to hold back when the other woman and your girlfriend are becoming sexually acquainted; it would be better to not have intercourse with the other woman this first time. That way there

will be less possibility of emotions like jealousy and possessiveness rearing their ugly heads mid-act—and making things weird the morning after.

Says Justin, a guy who, with his girlfriend and a friend, wound up in a 12-hour round of sexual indulgence, "We spent that night until the late morning rolling around, then watching TV, then eating cold pizza, then rolling around." Justin didn't have straight-up sex with the friend—nor with his girlfriend—that night but says that isn't the point. "Fooling around and having two women rub their naked bodies all over me, while we jerked each other off for hours and hours, was more than satisfying."

So what about me and my man Fred? No, we haven't done it yet. But I told him to ease off, so now, of course, I'm cool enough with the idea to joke about it in a tellingly casual way. I'll point to a woman walking down the street and be like, "Do you think she's hot? Should we do her?" It's part of a sexy game—and one I think may go further…if he can just let me take my own sweet time.

5. Read her hips with your lips. If she's enjoying what you're doing, she may run her hands through your hair or start chanting like a Gregorian monk. Or maybe she'll just lie there with her arms over her head in a pleasure coma with a big gooey grin on her face. Either way, since you can't see much right now, you'll have to rely on what's in front of you to know if she likes what you're doing.

Start by keeping your head still and observing her pelvic "platform" as she moves her body around you. If she's pushing forward into your face, she wants more pressure with your tongue. If she's inching backward, that means it might be too much and you should ease up. If she's sliding side to side, you might be off target and she's helping you relocate her bull's-eye. Whatever it is, she wants to let you know what feels good (and what doesn't) without having to *spell it out* for you, so take a moment and let her body be your guide.

> **WHEN SHE IS GOING DOWN, DON'T LIE THERE LIKE SOME SLEAZY HOLLYWOOD EXECUTIVE.**

6. Play to have fun—not to win. Women suspect that most guys approach oral sex like the game Doom. You're a mercenary grunt running through an extraterrestrial moon base with demons hurling fireballs as you attempt to survive monster heads about to engulf you in flames. On behalf of women everywhere, I urge you to consider oral sex more like a game of Myst. You land on an island where all around you are mysterious objects you have to figure out in order to unlock the island's big secret. No explosives, nothing to kill, just your skill, patience, and the willingness to play for hours.

That being said, the approximate amount of down time the average woman will expect you to clock in is a good 15 to 20 minutes—30 max. "Maybe I'll want to wait and climax during intercourse," explains Melissa, 27, a graduate student in Gainesville, Florida, "or maybe I'm enjoying his ministrations, but I just can't seem to get there that way." Whatever is going on, after you've hit that 20 to 30 mark, head back up and give her the "good waiter" treatment: Ask, Is she enjoying herself? Would she care for a glass of water? Would she like the check, or Is there something else you can do for her? She'll let you know what she wants to do next...and it just might be you.

Her Big Trip Downtown

A great blow job can be a whole lot more than the lie-back-and-do-nothing event you've come to expect, says *Maxim* editor Amy Spencer. It starts with giving her a reason to enjoy it. Why worry about *her* pleasure when this is *your* blow job? Because the more she enjoys it, the more she'll do it. And the more she does it...you following me, boys?

1. Hold the pickles. For most girls, hearing about blow jobs in the high school locker room is more horrifying than the acting in *Starship Troopers:* You have to deep-throat him, hide your teeth, and pump your head up and down faster than a

president's yes-man? Most women didn't enjoy that very first time they lip-launched a man's missile; the truth is, some still don't enjoy it. Why? Maybe it makes her gag. Maybe she feels like she's degrading herself. Maybe she doesn't like being told what to do, or hates the taste of semen, or thinks your crotch smells like sour milk.

The only way you'll know is by asking her. "I used to hate blow jobs until I went down on this one guy who told me I didn't have to swallow," says Beth, 21, a property management assistant in Des Moines, Iowa. "I realized that it wasn't the blow job I didn't like; it was having guys come in my mouth." She thought she didn't like the burger deluxe, when it was really the special sauce she could do without. Isn't it worth the effort to find out what a special order could do?

2. Don't ask, don't tell. Your best bet? *Don't ask for it.* If you don't know a woman well, there's really no way to do it without sounding like the pizza guy in a cheesy porno. "I was making out with this guy in his car on our first date when he said, 'Suck my cock,'" says Kim, 35, a musician in Chicago. "I

AFTER THE LOVIN', WHATEVER YOU DO, DO NOT JUMP UP AND THROW ON YOUR PANTS.

was so repulsed by what he said that I didn't go out with him again...and I certainly didn't *suck* anything." In general, saying things like "Blow me" and "Lick my dick" or pushing her head down forcefully is about as big a turn-on as a photo of a naked man on a red shag carpet with a cowboy hat hanging from his schlong.

"Look, I'm old enough to know that guys like blow jobs," says Lauren, 34, a lawyer in Washington, D.C. "I'll get to it when I feel comfortable." And anyway, telling her to do it takes some of the fun out of it—it's like asking for a lap dance at your own bachelor party. She's going to do it eventually, but she wants to take the driver's seat and shift you into high gear without you dropping the green flag. What you *can* do is tell her how hot she makes you and hope she gets the hint.

Or, here's a novel idea: Go down on her first. Citing Bible Belt wisdom, do unto others as you would have done unto you. Basic, sure, but it works. If you take the poontang plunge, it tells her you're a team player who has no intention of leaving her panting and unsatisfied. "Basically, if he goes down on me first, I find it inspirational," says Sharon, 26, an artist in New York City. "I will be his *slave* after that."

And there's the energy boost to consider. "I get so wet and revved when a guy gives me oral sex, I could run a marathon afterward!" says Clio, 25, an actress in Los Angeles. "It's like, 'Hey, you went down on me—now you get a Scooby snack too!'"

3. Baby, remember my name. Sure, the beauty of the blow job is that you don't have to do any work—you can hang up the humping hips, free your forearms, and save your sweat for the stair climber. But tuning out and folding your hands

behind your head like an ad for a Jamaican beach resort is not going to make the penis polish pleasurable for her.

One thing you can try is touching her. And I don't mean sticking your fingers into all the open cracks; while a little twat-tickling can be a turn-on for some, most women say they can't concentrate on giving head if they're receiving it at the same time. I mean touch her tenderly: Run your fingers softly along her back and shoulders, stroke her face, and play with her hair. (Nine out of ten women agree: The hair thing is guaranteed to melt her li'l heart.) Touching her sweetly will make her feel more special and less like a substitute for a blowup doll. And don't ever grab her head and drive it like a jackhammer on your piece of work. As one resentful woman put it, "That's the best way to get it bitten off."

SIZE DOES MATTER, BUT MAYBE NOT AS MUCH AS YOU THINK. IT'S CREATIVITY OVER SIZE ALMOST EVERY TIME.

Also, make it clear it's *her* you like, not just her popsicle practice. You can start by saying her name: Whisper it, groan it—stutter it if that's all you can muster. "One guy I was dating actually chanted my name when he got really hot," says Beth. "I felt like I was on the last stretch of the big race, with fans on the sidelines cheering for me. How could I not come through with a big finale?" Adds Claire, 31, a child psychologist in Lincoln, Nebraska: "One boyfriend used to reach down and move the hair out of my face, saying he wanted to see me while I blew him. I loved that—I felt like his personal porn star."

And, if she's making your bacon fry, tell her how great it feels, how this is the best you've ever felt (leave out the part "...in the last 10 minutes"), and let loose with an occasional "Ohmygodohmygodohmygod." Add how gorgeous she is, how great it is to be lying in bed beside her, and what you've got in mind for dessert. "I love it when they start telling you what they want to do to you while you're pleasing them," says Clio. "Like, 'I want to make you feel as good as you're making me feel.' That's always a winner."

But what if it's just not working? What if you've gotten a warmer reception from a raw rib eye? Time to lose the skittishness and communicate what you like. She doesn't have her nose nuzzled in your 'nads for nothin'—she *wants* to make it work. If you feel comfortable enough, tell her exactly what you want her to do ("Grab that part with your hand") and once she's on course, encourage her with simple directives ("A little lower, yeah, a little faster—yeah, just like that"). Or, disguise your desires in a fantasy: Tell her to pretend she's licking an ice-cream cone, or sucking on a straw. She knows what it's like to have a guy feverishly rubbing *her* an inch off the mark, so she'll appreciate knowing the spots that make *you* melt. If it's easier, acknowledge when she's doing something right, like the Hotter/Colder game you played as a kid: The closer she gets to your spout o' gold, the hotter you tell her she is—in words, moans, or Morse code. But watch how you say it. "One guy I went down on talked to me like a sports coach," remembers Catherine, 27, a teacher in Hoboken, New Jersey. "He actually *patted* me on the head and said, 'That's right, baby. Keep it up; you're doin' good.' I mean, encouragement is nice, but save the 'way to go' crap for your baseball buddies!"

And by all means, if she's hurting you, tell her right away. There's nothing worse than a woman hearing that her nails have been scratching you...for 20 minutes. A simple "Ooh, I'm a little sensitive there" or "Just a bit lighter" can make all the difference. Take it from Jen, 29, an editor in New York City: "I was dating this guy for four months before he told me that my teeth were rubbing him raw every time I gave him head!"

4. Don't push for the big gulp. We know: You want to believe that a woman thinks your semen is the most delicious thing she's ever tasted and that she'd feel empty inside if she didn't lick up every last drop. Well, guys, if your jam was that good, it'd be on the shelf next to Smuckers. Many of my girlfriends don't *mind* the taste—but I haven't met a woman yet who looks forward to tasting it.

Your spooge, whether bitter, sweet, or salty, has a consistency like egg whites, phlegm, and Elmer's glue mixed together. (Great for papier-mâché, not so great for mouthwash.) Which is why your best bet's to let her know when you're about to come and then let *her* decide what she'll do. She may keep doing what she's doing, or she might prefer to finish you off with a hand job and watch your geyser go up from afar. The key is letting her decide. "This one girl I know," informs Clio, "said a guy didn't tell her he was coming, and when he ejaculated in her mouth, she spit it in his face."

Keep the experience enjoyable, and she may decide some adventurous (and probably drunk) night to bring you to blow job bliss by swallowing. Until then, don't force her. In fact, don't even ask. "This one guy kept telling me how much sexier it would be if I could swallow it," says Betsy, 31, a researcher in Boston. "But when I tried, I ended up gagging, running to the bathroom, and dry-heaving over the toilet. How's sexy is *that*?"

5. Know that it ain't over. As with sex, try your best not to pass out right after the blast. Pull her up to you, cuddle with her, stroke her hair (can't stress that hair thing enough), and kiss her, which tells her you don't mind swapping fluids. "Keep something around for me to spit into or clean up with," says Jamie, 26, a bartender in Key West, Florida. "Not like a spittoon, but a bath towel or a box of tissues. And have a glass of water on the nightstand—or better yet, offer to get me one!" Then, whether or not she really made your joint jump five minutes after she has finished, tell her how great it was. Tell her again before you both fall asleep. Thank her when you wake up, and call her at work to say you can't stop thinking about it. Because any woman who feels she's made an impression like *that* will want to come back for an encore. In a few weeks she'll be playing your instrument like Jerry Lee Lewis.

Well, that's about it, boys. Now that you've heard me and 100 girlfriends divulge our secrets about everything from how we let a guy know we like him from five bar stools away to what we really (and I mean really) want in bed, it's time to take your new, totally unfair edge out into the world and start using it against us. (Hey, wait a minute, what were we thinking?). I'd like to say we opened our pink diaries to you guys out of the kindness of our hearts, but the truth is, I was able to get all these women to help out because we're just as tired as you are of the confusion between the sexes. So if baring our dirty little secrets can help cut through the clutter of mixed signals, clear up the bad communications (and improve our sex lives!), that's a good deal all around. We hope it was as good for you as it was for us.

Love and kisses,
Leslie Yazel

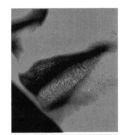